If I talk a little wild, forgive me;
I had it from my father.

Shakespeare: King Henry VIII, iv, 26.

Lern yerself SCOUSE

Volume 2:

The ABZ of Scouse by Linacre Lane, B.Sc. (Bachelor of Scouse)

"How to talk Proper on Merseyside"
edited by Fritz Spiegl and published by
SCOUSE PRESS LIVERPOOL L8 3SB

Liverpool's Oldest-established Publisher of
Local Humour and Local History - founded in 1965.
Telephone 0151-727 2727   Facsimile 0151-727 7272
Postal, Telephone or Fax enquiries only: there is no showroom.

First published 1966

© Linacre Lane and Scouse Press

Printed in China

Cacology: Faulty vocabulary or pronunciation.
(Greek: *kakos*, bad, *logos*, speech.)

Chambers's 20th Century Dictionary.

Foreword

LERN YERSELF SCOUSE—the title of the phrase book to which this volume acts as a companion—is in the argot with which it deals. It does not invite the reader to teach himself, because no natural-born speaker of Scouse is taught or teaches himself anything. He *lerns hisself*. In his very toddlerhood his mother *lerned* him, usually by bawling in loud, adenoidal tones, *"I'll lern yer ter act like that!"* and following it up with a series of bloodcurdling threats. The Scouser mother is the kind of well-meaning but muddle-minded parent who restrains her brat from wandering into the path of traffic by screaming at the top of her rasping voice, *"If yer gets yerself kilt I'll bloody well merder yer!"* As you will discover if you seek on the right page, *kilt* means killed.

A Scouser is a Merseysider who conducts his ordinary, everyday conversations in Scouse complete with the correct cold-in-the-head intonation and to the accompaniment of all the appropriate nods, winks and elbow-digs. A Scouser is not necessarily a Liverpudlian though the odds are in favour of it. He could come from anywhere within a fifteen mile radius of Moby Dick, which is a famous statue much admired for its generous proportions. The concentration of Scouse is greatest in an off-centre area covering about ten square miles but there are large patches of irredeemable practitioners in new housing estates towards and beyond the perimeter of the city.

It should not be (but is) necessary to say that not all

Merseysiders speak Scouse. Some come from places like Llanbrynmair or Llanfaircaereinion or Penrhyndeuddraeth and are able to pronounce a mysterious foreign word like *twlldene*. Some speak Glasgow or Edinburgh Scotch or plain, ordinary *och awa'* Scotch. Some Merseysiders gabble together in Swahili, Urdu, Hindi and Tamil while those with no teeth are alleged to speak in gum Arabic. A few address a respected elder as *Ah Pak*, meaning Old Uncle. There are broad-vowelled *Ee, lad!* Lancashire types and no doubt there may be a few West Hartlepoolers who go berserk when asked, "Who hung the monkey?"

Above all there is the pride and joy of official and socially conscious Merseyside, namely, many enclaves of people who *talk proper* or think they *talk proper* or are believed to *talk proper*. This last category of good folk is trotted out and exhibited with monotonous regularity to prove that all Merseyside talks *proper* and that anyone who thinks otherwise is a dirty black Protestant liar. The challenge is met with extra-special alacrity if it happens to emanate from Manchester, a dirty dump where some people speak Mancunian, a mixture of Failsworth Lancashire, Lower Broughton Yiddish and Moss Side Pidgin.

The influences that created Scouse are more mixed than the ancestry of many Liverpool dogs, and that is saying a lot. The oldest and most basic one is embedded in the conditions attending the Industrial Revolution. That was a time when labour was drawn from the land

and into the "dark, satanic mills". As machinery developed so also did the demand for skilled or semi-skilled workers. This caused an automatic sorting-out process among the employable. Those who had skills or were mentally capable of acquiring skills gravitated towards centres where they were most needed and security of employment seemed best assured; these became the working force upon which was founded the prosperity of great industrial conurbations like those of the Sheffield and Birmingham areas.

This left a large residue of would-be workers who lacked the ability to acquire skills or, being shiftless, lacked the ambition. Some were too dull-witted to pass muster, others too mentally lazy to make the effort. Therefore they sought work of a kind with which they could cope, wherever they could find it, and rapidly expanding Merseyside was a Mecca for such people.

As the country's industrial complexes expanded and the export trade swelled with it, so Merseyside grew as a port and distribution centre more concerned with the handling of goods than the manufacture of them. This situation had great appeal to individuals unable to tell a vertical drill from a turret lathe but well able to hump crates and sacks up or down a ship's gangway or whack the arse off a carthorse—hence, possibly, the Scouse nickname of *whacker,* though most people now seem to prefer the spelling *wacker.**

* See *"Lern Yerself Scouse" for another theory.*

Of course, with this influx of the energetic but none-too-bright came people of a different calibre for different reasons. Scots, sniffing the lovely odour of an easy groat, charged over the Border and confiscated banks, insurance companies and ships' engine-rooms. Welsh filtered in to open little shops that in some cases grew into departmental stores. Chinese formed colonies originally derived from shipping connections in Hong Kong and Singapore. And so it went on for about a century and a half during most of which Merseyside's prosperity depended mainly—though not wholly—upon the crate-handlers, the sack-carriers and the horse-whackers, or in the most up-to-date cliché, the "service industries".

Let us face the awful fact: it is from the uneducated and in some respects uneducatable stratum of Merseyside life that Scouse has arisen and developed. To a great extent it is the language of the ignorant. Some outsiders view it with pity, some with ill-concealed contempt, some wholeheartedly approve it on the grounds that it is always good for a laugh. There may be much to be said for the latter viewpoint if one accepts a well-known humorist's explanation of the success of so many Merseyside comedians: *"If you live in Liverpool you must either laugh yourself sick or burst into tears."*

Liverpool is by no means as bad as that opinion implies; on the other hand, it is a hell of a long way from being the cultural paradise that some of its snootier citizens like to pretend. Indeed, the twanging, yowling uproar that was its recent contribution to the lunatic though lucrative fringe of music can be described as typically and inevitably Liverpool. Even more typical is the fact that Liverpool takes perverted pride in it. What is the first shrine at which the visitor to Liverpool now worships? Allerton Hall, where William Roscoe fought for the abolition of slavery? Jesse Hartley's Albert Dock, that breath-taking, unique example of early Victorian Dock Architecture? Wood & Wyatt's Town Hall or the exquisite Queen Anne symmetry of the old Blue Coat School? None of these. Be he a dollar-spending tourist or publicity-seeking politician, the first place he makes for is a dank, sweaty, underground warehouse where "The Liverpool Sound" was born—probably the most successful mass bamboozle since the virgin birth.

But can one blame the visitor? There are hardly any places of architectural or historic interest left in the city. Most of them have disappeared within living memory to make way for development—much of it quite appallingly ugly. The Liverpool Town Books bear melancholy witness to an unceasing record of destruction-in-the-name-of-progress, the words *"It is resolved this day to demolish . . ."* appearing with monotonous frequency on the pages covering the last two centuries. The process, alas, has not yet been halted, but the methods employed in recent decades have if anything been more insidious: the technique being to allow old property to be neglected, ravaged by vandals, and then to demolish it as being "an eyesore and beyond repair".

In its place is then built an office block, public house or petrol station (usually within a few yards of an existing office block, public house or petrol station). Liverpool is well on the way to becoming a Chicago or Detroit of N.W. England. A city that loses its heritage also loses its character.

But to return to Scouse. As a dialect—for it *is* a dialect and not just a regional accent—Scouse has many curious features worthy of the study of anyone who takes a scientific interest in aboriginal speech-forms. For example, the true Scouser has a linguistic blind-spot with respect to the past tense. Therefore he plays it by ear, so to speak. He substitutes *seen* for "saw", *done* for "did", *clumb* for "climbed", *fruz* for "frozen", *kilt* for "killed", *scairt* for "scared", and so on. Scousers long accustomed to the phrase: *"I seen 'im!"* (which they regard as perfect English as used in Buckingham Palace), are quick to detect the low educational standard of the boob who says: *"I seed 'im!"*

No Scouser can be convinced in a month of Sundays that a sentence employing a double negative is, in fact, a positive statement. Hence the Scouser will frequently utter passionate words that mean the precise opposite of what he is trying to say. One delinquent Scouser reached what may well be the all-time record for use of negatives with this statement offered to a bench of magistrates: *"It weren't me wot done it. I tole 'im I didn't want no part of nuttin' ter do wit' nuttin' about it."* Fortunately the magistrates, long experienced in the deviations of Scouse, were able to translate this mess of nasal whinings into a protestation of innocence—and probably a damned lie. But even the learned Liverpool lawyers appear sometimes to experience difficulties in this field, as the following cutting from a Liverpool newspaper shows:

> "I think it inexcusable it was not said this clothing had no trace of petrol on it.
> "I hope this practice of not mentioning negative findings is not common and will never be repeated."
> He told the accused.

Scouse is unique, highly evocative and often deliciously witty, but no-one can say that it is beautiful. Perhaps the very reason for its present popularity is to be found in the current cult of almost sado-masochistic ugliness: "op." paintings that are "fun" because they hurt the eye; plays that are "amusing" because babies are murdered on the stage; and music which is physically painful to listen to.*

It is not only beat music that assaults the ear. Invidious as it may be to single out individual composers I'd like to put on record that after each performance of Messiaen's "Oiseaux Exotiques" every single performer, myself included, suffered from a splitting headache.—F.S.

But of course Scouse is more than a fashion that is artificially generated by the PRO and blessed by the switched-on, with-it Sunday supplements. We suggest that it evolved itself from a variety of outside influences and this inevitably means that much of it has been borrowed from other and sometimes faraway sources. The difficulty in tracing real origins is such that it is any man's guess how much of a Scouser's language is his own and how much somebody else's. A word like *scuffer* (policeman), for example, appears to be peculiar to Merseyside and therefore may be assumed to be pure Scouse. On the other hand, *char* (tea), is an Indian Army term that outdates Scouse by at least half a century. The fairly recent tendency to use *thundermug* (chamber-pot), suggests an American importation while *bushwha* (rubbish, nonsense), is Outback Australian. No doubt the perceptive reader will recognise odd words and phrases long regarded as the private property of the Navy, Merchant Navy or anyone else from whom the more emphatic forms of speech may be stolen. There is nothing unusual about this; all languages enrich themselves from other languages. Scouse differs only in one respect, namely, that the average Scouser firmly believes in his linguistic virginity. He is quite capable of appropriating any long-used word or phrase that strikes his fancy and, at later date, swearing before God that the original user stole it from Scouse.

We have seen no reason to exclude Anglo-Saxon vulgarisms from this work, the only qualification for inclusion being that they are characteristic of, though not necessarily exclusive to, Liverpool speech. Without them, indeed, Scouse would be reduced to the pale level of Palladium comics. By the same token, we have included certain Scouse folk-jokes where they illustrate —albeit inadequately in print—the kind of repartee Liverpudlians delight in.

We are grateful to many readers of 'Lern Yerself Scouse' who kindly pointed out omissions from that book, in particular Dr. Denis Chapman, Mrs Mildred Mordaunt, Messrs. E. Freeman, Harry Hughes, Gerry Jones, Robert B. Milligan, and David Prole. Many of their suggestions appear in the following pages.

A

abbadabba: Incomprehensible language; any form of speech regarded as meaningless gabble. As in **I could'n' make 'ead ner tail o' that feller, 'e guv me a lotter abbadabba.**

abyssinia then: I will see you again sometime.

act soft an' I'll buy yer a tin whistle: Being silly will gain you nothing.

Other similar expressions: "act soft an' I'll buy yer a coal-yard"; "act soft an' I'll drag yer ter ther grotter" (Christmas grotto); "act soft an' yez can 'ave a ride on me back step" (of a bicycle); "act soft an' they'll drill an 'ole in it" (meaning one's skull).

ackers: Money. **whur's the ackers?:** Where is the money?

ain't even gotter shillun fer ther meter: Hard up, penniless.

This phrase is greatly favoured when trying to cadge, in whining tones, from shopkeepers, priests, various charities, the National Assistance Board or anyone thought of as a mug.

ain't laughed so 'ard since me old man broke 'is leg: I had a long, loud, hearty laugh.

Other similar expressions are: "ain't laughed so 'ard since Joe Soap got stuck in ther petty"; "ain't laughed so 'ard since Uncle Willie lost 'is balls."

alaira: A children's skipping game based upon the recital of **one, two, three, alaira!**

'Ail Mury: A prayer, a penance, a Catholic.

Ali or Alley: A barber. Derived from *Ali Baba*.

alley-band: A children's band composed of performers on folded privet-leaves, hair-combs and biscuit-tins. *Also "Foo-Foo Band".*

all-in wrestler: A person who boasts of his sexual prowess.

allus simster: Always seems to.

anyroad: in any case.

anny ur-GAR?: A street cry meaning **any old rags?**

A less used variation is "anny ur-GAR, bols, buns?" meaning "any old rags, bottles or bones?"

Anytime Annie: A prostitute.

are yez lookin' fer a buncher daffs?: Are you seeking trouble or trying to start a fight?
The reference is to daffodils in the sense of cheap flowers for a funeral.

argify: To argue. **'e'd argify the 'ind leg offer donkey.**

argy-bargy: A silly dispute; a quarrel.

ar kid: A brother, usually a younger one, but occasionally older or even a sister. **'Oo's ther feller what done ar kid?** Who is the man who beat up my brother?

ar Mury: Our Mary.

ar soljers wenter war: A patriotic but vulgar folk-song once popular with Scouser children who howled it along back alleys to the accompaniment of clashing cymbals (dustbin lids).

One version of this song is:
  "Our sol, Our sol, our soljers went ter fight
  With pis, with pis, with pistols at their side." etc.
The collector of useless information may like to know that the tune to which these words are usually sung occurs in Busoni's Piano Concerto. Its appearance in such incongruous surroundings caused much amusement, at any rate in the orchestra, when this work was played in Liverpool. But Busoni did visit Liverpool not long before he wrote the work . . .

artnoon: Afternoon. **Whur's yer goin' this artnoon?**

as daft as soft Mick: Very, very silly.

as relaxed as a cow-flop: Very much at ease; bone idle.

'atches is off, de: The pub is open.

Atlas: Sardonic name given to an undersized, weedy individual.

avvy: afternoon.

aw cheese: An expression of disappointment or dissatisfaction.

awkard: Awkward. **Yer as awkard as yer 'alf-daft Da.**

axe: To ask. As in **did 'e axe yer about it?**

aye: The affirmative with a slight emphasis. As in **aye, I've 'ad a few jars** (of beer). However, **aye** is easily the most flexible word in Scouse. There is the **aye**-incredulous, the **aye**-sympathetic, the **aye**-sardonic, the **aye**-assertive and twenty or more other versions. Two Scousers can conduct a long conversation with one of them saying nothing but **aye** with various inflexions. See *Lern Yerself Scouse*.

B

back crack: A back alley.

Cf. "Ye Olde Cracke", a not-so-olde but well-known alehouse in an alley in Liverpool 8.

bad breath: A spicy fruit-loaf properly called by its Welsh name of **bara brith.**

bad weather fer brass monkeys: Very cold weather.

Based on a folk-joke concerning the disastrous effect of low temperatures upon the anatomy of monkeys, even those made of brass.

bag: In theory, a prostitute, but more often used as a term of abuse. **That owd bag!** merely expresses derision, contempt or dislike. When dragged indoors by its mother, a Scouser child is quite capable of screaming **lemme be, yer rotten owd bag!**

bags: Lots of; plenty. **bags a scoff:** plenty of food.

bailiff: Any person who presses for payment of a debt.

bald as a melling (melon): Completely bald.

balls ter you, I'm fireproof: I am completely indifferent; I couldn't care less.

Band of Hope Street: The Royal Liverpool Philharmonic Orchestra.

bangers: Sausages. Hence **bangeroo:** a pig.

banner-socket: A navel.

Cf. The frequent "marches" of the Orangemen (the Protestants) and the "walks" of their Catholic rivals. Both factions carried banners whose poles could, in emergencies, be used as weapons.

banny-mug: Pieces of broken pottery used by children as currency in games and for making chalk marks on pavements.

barmisod: A term of abuse, as in **I wooden be seen dead wit' that barmisod.**

barney: A dispute; a heated argument.

barrer: A street trader's handcart. **barrer-girl:** a female street trader of any age up to ninety. **Keep yer thievin' 'ands off me barrer:** I don't trust you any more than you can trust me.

bash: An effort; an attempt; **on ther bash:** on a sexual spree; **have a bash:** have a go.

bastard: Not always used insultingly; sometimes in admiration, combined perhaps with a playful punch on the jaw or chest, as in **yer a rill owd bastard—yer owd bastard!**

batter: To smack or slap.
The love-call of a Scouser parent to its offspring may sometimes be "if yer don' come in at wunst I'll batter ther bloody daylights outer yer!"

bayoes: Public Baths.
Cf. Italian "bagno" and 18th-century English "bagnio".

bayonet practice: Sexual intercourse.
Cf. "Mutton dagger" : penis.

beady-eyed bastard: An inquisitive male, a nosey-parker. The female of the species is a **beady-eyed bitch.**

bed-mates: Fleas. **'E were fair crawlin' wit' bed-mates:** he had a lot of fleas.

bed wetter: An early riser.

beer money: Unemployment allowance. **Me owd feller ain't in, 'e's gone fer 'is beer money.**

bellers ter mend: Short of breath (i.e. "bellows to

mend"—an old street cry).

belt: An effort; a blow. Also sexual intercourse.

bent: Broken; smashed; completely destroyed.
A smashed shop-window or a wrecked car are said to have been "bent".

berd: As **bint**.

berd-cage: A girls' school; a nunnery; any room or hall holding an assembly of females.

berd-watcher: A man who ogles the opposite sex.

Berk'ned: The Borough of Birkenhead.

Berky types or **Berky bums:** Derisory terms for youths living in **Birkenhead.**

berry: A beret but sometimes any old out-of-shape hat.

bevvied: Drunk. The Scouser's favourite excuse for an act of hooliganism is **I wuz bevvied.**
Cf. Latin "bibere", to drink, but more likely from Bevington Bush, where the Bevington Brewery once stood. And, of course, "beverage".

biddies: Lice. **Teacher sent me 'ome; she sez me 'ead's full of biddies.**

biddy: An elderly woman of scruffy appearance. **Owd biddy:** old woman.

Perhaps a diminution of "Bridget", the generic name for Irish women.

big blow: A braggart; a bombastic person. **That feller's jus' a big blow.**

big-ears: An inquisitive person; a nosey-parker. As in **yer mind yer own sufrance (sufferance), big-ears!**

big-'ead: A term of abuse. See **cow-'ead.**

bint: A girl or young woman. Less used than **judy.**

An unadulterated importation from the Arabic, meaning "girl".

bits: Small pieces and left-over ends of meat used for making cheap stew, including **lobscouse** (scouse). Also over-cooked fragments of potato and batter sold as a by-product by some fish-and-chip shops.

blackie: A police van. Derived from **Black Maria.**

Also called a "paddy wagon"; or "battle taxi" if of the Jeep/Land-Rover type.

blind: A word used for emphasis as in **'e wooden take a blind bit er notice of me** or **nobody could get a blind bit er sense outer 'im.**

blind as a one-legged ref: Thoughtless; unobservant; stupid. The reference is to a football referee.

blind scouse: Lobscouse made without meat.

blind man, blinder or **blindy:** A person addicted to the drinking of wood alcohol, surgical or methylated spirits, which often cause blindness.

block: To have sexual intercourse.

block: The noun, as distinct from the verb, means a head. **I done me block;** I went off my head; I lost my temper.

blocker: A bowler or derby hat. Also called a **funeral** or **burial hat.** Less frequently a **plug-hat.**
Hence "blocker, blockerman" = a foreman.

blocks: Compressed cubes of coal-dust, sawdust and cement used to keep household fires going.

blood-olly: An alley or marble made of red-streaked stone.

bloody 'ero: Ironical term for anyone who joins the armed forces for full length of service or for anyone who volunteers for a task disliked by everyone else.

blower: A telephone. **Give 'im ther griff on ther**

blower: telephone the information to him.

blow-through: Sexual intercourse.

bobby dazzler: Anything considered good-looking, attractive, especially a girl.

bogies: Large pottery marbles.

bog-trotter or **bog-hopper:** An Irishman, usually not from Cork or Dublin.

Bollicky Fifth, Ther: The 5th (Rifle) Battalion, The King's (Liverpool) Regiment.
Derived from a vulgar marching song beginning "O, ther Bollicky Fifth er a derty lot, they lost their colours at Aldershot", etc., etc. This is bawled to the tune of the battalion march, a lively jig entitled "I'm Ninety-Nine".

bonzer: Very good; excellent. Less used than **ther gear.**

boozer: A public house.

boozery: A brewery.

booze-hound: A persistent drunkard.

booze-jerk or **jerker:** A bartender.

booze-moke: A brewery-horse.

booze-up: A drinking bout. **Ev'ry Satdy night we 'ad a bloody good booze-up.**

boozin' wit' ther bugs: Solitary drinking at home.

boxed: Boxed in one's coffin or actually buried.

boxer: A coffin-maker. Sometimes applied to an undertaker.

break eleven, to: To be caught in a nefarious act.

Derived from the so-called Eleventh Commandment: "Thou shalt not be found out".

breaks: Broken, defective or damaged biscuits sold cheaply, usually from a crate or barrel.

brew: A slope, rise or hill. **oop ther brew:** Up the slope.

The Lancashire pronunciation of "brow".

brew-up: To make a pot or can of tea, preferably in the employer's time.

bright: Well; healthy. Used in a negative sense as in **I'm not too bright terday.** See also **smart** and **clever.**

brownie: A male prostitute. Also called a **joy-boy, ship's Mary,** etc., etc.

Brutal Bootle where ther bugs wear clogs: Derisory description of a county borough at the north end of Merseyside.

Brutal types or **Brutal scruffs**: Derogatory terms for youths living in Bootle.

Buckingham Palace: An old-established boarding-house known as **Champion Whaite's,** located at Mile End, Liverpool.

buggers about like a fartna bottle: Said of a hopeless muddler, a restlessly busy person.

bunce: extra pay, bonus.

bur fax: The essentials; the bare facts. **I told 'im ther bur fax an' 'e went crackers.**

Bush, Ther: Bevington Bush, a Liverpool street.

bushed: Lost, bewildered. Similar terms are **raddled** and **muzzied.**

bushwha: Nonsense; idle talk; a foolish rumour.
Derived from the Australian "bush-wire", speculative gossip.

Cf. also "Latrinograph" (Army slang): hearsay transmission of news.

bust a gut: To get very angry, as in **I could a bust a gut.** Also to work extremely hard, as in **I 'ad ter slog at it until I could a bust a gut.**

Busy Lizzie: A busybody; a persistent interferer in other people's affairs.

bull or **bullsh:** Nonsense; silly talk; unnecessary formality.
From an Army slang word meaning "unnecessary chores".

bullamacow: Corned beef. This word is an African importation, seldom used, but then ironically.

bulwark of Britain: Derisory description applied to a weedy, undersized individual.

bum: To beg, borrow or cadge, as in **can I bum a cupfulla sugar fer ther time bean?**

bum-droops: Condition attributed to persons long in the trunk and short in the legs. Also called **duck's disease.**

bumstarver: A short, ill-cut jacket.
Also "bumfreezer"; in Victorian times ladies' bustles were known as "arse-coolers".

bumsucker: A person who curries favour; a toady.

bunce: Dockers' slang for extra pay (i.e. bonus).

bundook: A rifle, shotgun or airgun. Applied ironically to an umbrella, especially when neatly folded.

bung or **bungole:** Cheese.

bun-oven: A top hat. **It were a rill posh wedd'n'—'e were wearin' stripey kecks an' a bun-oven.**

butty: A slice of bread smeared with edible fat described as butter or margarine. **Batty-butty:** A sandwich filled with an unidentifiable paste. **Chip-butty:** a sandwich containing fried potatoes. **Dip-butty:** a slice of bread dipped in warm fat, usually bacon fat. **Dog-butty:** a corned beef sandwich. **Dry-butty** or **gerk-butty:** a slice of plain, uncoated bread. **Gip-butty:** bread dipped in **gippo** or gravy. **Jam-butty:** bread smeared with jam, not necessarily with any accompanying grease. **Tripe-butty:** a sandwich containing cold tripe. **Welsh-butty:** a sandwich containing cheese and sliced raw onion.

C

Cabbage Hall Yank: A youth who tries to behave like, or pretends to be, an American. Also called a **Wells Fartole type.**

caidy or **straw caidy:** A straw boater hat. Also called a **cheese cutter.**

canary cake: Plain, saffron-coloured slab-cake.

can-lad: A boy who makes tea for workers. Also a lowly, ill-paid job, hence the complaint **jer take me fer a bloody can-lad?**

can't tell Paddy's Market from St. George's 'All: Said of a person considered dull-witted.

Other similar phrases are: "can't tell Tuesday from a bull's foot"; "can't tell a yard er rope from a flat pint" (of beer); "can't tell Liverpool from Preston North End", etc., etc.

carnival ribbons: Toilet rolls.

These are often used by Merseyside football supporters as outsized streamers.

cassoona: A mythical individual alleged to have teeth in his backside and blamed for biting buttons off railway carriage seats.

Cast Iron Shore, Ther or **Ther Cazzy:** A rocky riverside shore at the southern end of Liverpool.

cat-kisser: An animal lover. Also called a **poodle-primper.**

Cat'licks: Roman Catholics.

chamber music: Lavatory noises. Also called **handle's water music.**

champion or **proper champion:** Very good, first-class, excellent. This is part of Lancashire dialect and less used than **ther gear.**

chapel-going bastard: A term of abuse.

char: Tea. **cuppachar:** A cup of tea.

cheeses, cheese: Mispronunciation of a blasphemous exclamation.

cheese cutter: A straw boater hat. See **caidy.**

cherry-bobs or **cherry-wobs:** A children's game in

which cherry stones are flipped at a rainwater-spout, or used as marbles substitutes.

chillun: Children. **I bin a good mother ter me chillun an' now they's bein' good ter me** is the self-satisfied boast sometimes made over a glass of stout.

Chinee: A Chinaman. Chin*ese* being considered already plural.

chinky chuck: Chinese food.

chippy: A fish-and-chip shop.

choker: A muffler; a working scarf, naturally often full of honest grime. **'im wit' ther clean choker** refers to a person regarded as uppish and suspected of nursing secret ambitions.

chooks: A term of affection applied ironically to any member of the opposite sex regardless of age or repulsiveness. Less used than **luv** but more often than **ducks.**

choss: Complete disorder, as in **it were absolute berluddy choss.** A mispronunciation of **chaos.**

chuck: To give. **chuck us ther tit:** Please be good

enough to pass me the milk. **chuck** also means food in the same sense as the Australian **tucker**. **Chuck-box:** a food container; a sandwich box. To **get chucked:** to have one's friendship or engagement abruptly terminated.

churs: Chairs. **whur's ther churs?:** Where are the chairs?

clappers: Figurative bells. **Goin' like ther clappers of hell:** moving very fast.

Clarence Mbongo: Applied to a Negro, especially if young and dressy.

clean mennal: Dotty; decidedly mad. As in **yer better watch that feller, 'e's clean mennal.**

clean-ther-pan: a primitive superstition like that of trying to avoid walking on the cracks between paving-stones. Only practised by males.

Although "clean-ther-pan" is known to practically every man and boy throughout the civilised world, it is apparently only in Liverpool that this harmless solitary sport has been given a name. There are no rules and no skill is required—the object of the game being to remove, by the most natural means at the player's disposal, any traces of previous use from the inside of sanitary ware.

clever: Well; in good health. Used in a negative sense

as in **I'm not too clever jus' now**. See **bright** and **smart**.

cloggie: A person who wears wooden clogs. This term is becoming obsolete, clogs being worn only for certain industrial purposes.

clonkers: Wooden clogs or heavy hobnailed boots. **I belted 'im wit' me clonkers**: I kicked him. **Clonkers** is also a contest in which opponents grip hands and kick each other with clogs until one admits defeat. Note the similarity to the Dutch word **klompers**.

clumb or **clum**: Climbed, as in **I clumb over ther wall**.

Coats 'n' 'Ats: A Liverpool departmental store properly called **C & A Modes, Ltd**.

cobs: Large lumps. As in **if I don't go 'ome ther gaffer'll knock cobs off me**.

cobbles: Cobblestones. **got nuts like cobbles** is said of a man considered big and powerful.

cod: Deceit; leg-pulling; tomfoolery. **Thassa lotter cod!**: I just don't believe it.

Coddy's Show: An old-established Punch and Judy

show run by a Liverpool family named **Codman,** all apparently possessing an hereditary title of "Professor".

Cold as a nun's bum: very cold indeed.

A riddle traditionally asked by older players of the Liverpool Philharmonic: "What are the two coldest things in the world?" A: A nun's bum and a solo on the viola. Riposte: "And the two most useless?" A: Father Bunloaf's goolies and a Vote of Thanks to the Orchestra."

Collitch: a college. **Collitch pudd'n:** a person who likes to be thought of as educated. **Ther Collitch:** Liverpool College or Liverpool Collegiate School.

comby: A motor-cycle combination.

come-overs: A Manx term for visiting holiday-makers, many of whom are from Merseyside. Also for immigrants to that island. The **come-overs** retaliate by calling themselves **go-backers.**

compost-flake: Herbal tobacco.

c'mon kid, let's creep: Invitation to the dance.

conny-onny: Condensed milk. Also called **stiff moo** and **stiff tit.**

cooee: A lover's lane or any dark alley in which

amatory exercises can be performed; **up ther cooee:** to be placed in a difficult or embarrassing position.

Corny dips: Cornwallis Street Public Baths.

corpy: A corporation house.

could eat a child wit' ther smallpox: Very, very hungry.

couldn' kick (or punch) an 'ole in a wet Ekker: Said of a person thought to be futile, feeble, lacking in punch.
"Ekker" refers to "The Liverpool Echo". Other similar phrases are: "couldn't fight 'is way outer a paper bag"; "couldn't 'it a fly in a pissus", etc., etc.

couldn' organise a booze-up in a brewery: Of a totally incompetent person.

coupler bob: Very cheap; a bargain, as in **it only cost me a coupler bob.** (Cf. **millyins** = very expensive).

cow-'ead: A simpleton; a yokel. Note resemblance to the Lancashire **keouw-yed,** a stupid fellow.

cozzy: A bathing costume.
"Let's see yer without yer cozzy" is an invitation to a Scouser maiden to give away what little is left of her all, even when fully dressed and nowhere near a bathing-place.

craggy bastard: A serious minded, somewhat severe person.

crapper or **crappus**: A lavatory.

crawl back inter yer 'ole: Shut up, go away. Other similar phrases are: **crawl back inter yer rat-'ole; flush yerself down ther pan,** etc., etc.

crawlin' in ther spew: Too drunk to stand.

cream poof or **poofter**: An effeminate male.

creep: A worthless person; a slob.

creepin' Jesus: Applied to a person who enjoys bad health or constant misfortune; somebody who solicits sympathy by wearing an air of patient martyrdom.

Crock, Ther: The Crocodile, an old-established Liverpool pub-cum-restaurant.

crown jewels: Injuries to the head.

crud: Rubbish; nonsense.

Count of Monte Cristo, Ther: A dressy man; a show-off.

The first word is often intentionally mispronounced.

curd: Lemon cheese.

cut: A canal. **A dip in ther cut:** a swim in the canal.

cutty: A bargee. Also a stubby type of clay pipe.

cutty shark: A small fish; a tiddler or stickleback caught in a canal.

"Cutty" = Scots for "short", as in "Cutty Sark", a short chemise.

D

dairty cairt'ns: Dirty curtains. **We live nex' ter ther 'ouse wit' ther dairty cairt'ns.**

dat's a dairty black Protisant lie!: The absolute ultimate in untruths, usually proclaimed as such in an hysterical shout.

dead: Used for emphasis, as in **it's dead easy** or **she's dead nuts on 'im.**

dead spit: Alike; similar to. **That ther kid's ther dead spit of 'is gramp.**

Debtors' Retreat, Ther: Derisory name for the county borough of **Wallasey**, Cheshire.

decked up like a bloody May-horse: Overdressed; wearing conspicuous or flamboyant attire.

The reference is to a May-day procession once held by Liverpool carters and their horses. Other similar phases are: "dressed up like a dog's dinner"; "decked up like a moony bride"; "done up like a bloody Christmas-tree"; "done up like Lady Muck of Muck Hall", etc., etc.

dekko: To see, look at, watch for. **'Ave a dekko:** have a look.
(From the Hindustani; originally army slang.)

dem boids: Sardonic take-off of American slang applied to the Liver birds atop the Royal Liver Building on the Pier Head, Liverpool.
They are also called "the shite-hawks" and are said to flap their wings whenever a virgin passes beneath them.

desert wellies: sandals.
See also "Jesus boots".

dick: A detective. **sly dick:** a store detective. **clever-dick:** a person regarded as too big for his boots.

dicker: A dog whose owner takes pride in its amorous successes. **Whur's ar dicker?:** where is our canine Casanova?

dicky-docker: A Rabbi.

dindin: Dinner. As in **t'rah well, I gotter push off fer me dindin.**
"The Guardian" (of Manchester) has published a dignified protest against this word. (Dinner = lunch. Tea = supper. Supper = A late-night snack.)

dirt-track rider: A sexual pervert.

dirty (pronounced **dairty** or **derty,** depending on

location): Used for emphasis, as in **a dairty big muck-up,** meaning a great mess. **Ther dairty thairties:** an age classification along with the naughty forties, nifty fifties, etc., etc. **dairty stinkin' rotten drunk:** very drunk indeed.

do: A party, an affair, a happening. **Are yez goin' ter ther do?:** are you going to the party?

d.o.a.: Applied to a person considered a cretin, a congenital idiot.
Derived from the hospital term "dead on arrival".

Dockers' Umbrella, Ther: The **Liverpool Overhead Railway,** now demolished.
Nickname derived from people's habit of sheltering under it during heavy rain.

dodger: Bread or sometimes crude cake. **Gimme a slice er dodger.**

dodgy: Unreliable, doubtful, risky. **a dodgy do:** a risky affair.

does yer mother know yer out?: A derisory challenge possibly inherited from the old song **Cecilia.**

dog: Corned beef. **dog wit' bite:** corned beef with mustard. **bitey dog butty**—a rare expression—a corned beef sandwich with plenty of mustard.

Dogs' 'Ome, Ther: Walton Jail. Also called **Ther Gurk, Joe Gerk, Ther Jug, Ther Nick, Ther Waldorf-Astoria, Ther Wally.**

doins (doings): Whatzits, thingumajigs. **Whur's ther doins?**: where are the necessary items?

doll: A woman. **owd doll**: an old woman.

dolled up fer a late wedd'n': Said of a flamboyantly dressed, no longer young, woman.

dolly or **dolly-peg** or **peggy**: A nearly obsolete wooden instrument used for churning washing in a tub.

Hence the solicitous enquiry about the cause of a black eye: "she clout yer wit' ther dolly?"

do me over, daddio: Female Scouser's equivalent of **chase me, Charlie.**

done: Did. **'e done it—I seen 'im**: He did it—I saw him.

donkeystone: A soft stone, creamy or light grey, used for colouring doorsteps and window-ledges. **as worn out as a donkeystone**: thoroughly exhausted.

don' cum ther rubber duck: Don't be silly (or childish).

don' fiddle-arse aroun': Don't waste time hanging about and doing nothing.

don' know if 'e's comin' or goin': Muddle-minded, witless. Other similar phrases are: **couldn't climb a ten-foot ladder; don't know Thairsday from brekfuss-time; don't know 'is arse from 'is elbow; can't tell 'is tits in a black sack,** etc., etc.

doss: To sleep. **Me ole man can't see yer now, 'e's 'avin' a doss.**

do ther mint, to: To break open and rob a gas or electric meter.

dowse it: Stop it, look out, make ready to run. See **get set.** To **keep dowse:** to keep watch, usually while some kind of illegal activity is taking place.

dozey: Slow-thinking, dull-witted. **Dozey-arsed bastard:** a stupid person.

down de 'atch: Your Health! Prosit! Skol! Cheers! etc.

d.p.: A discharged prisoner.

drack: A person with prominent or projecting teeth. Derived from **Dracula.**

drain me 'taters: urinate. Also **pump me bilges** (nautical).

drippy: Slovenly, dishevelled, unattractive.

drug: Dragged. **Ther scuffers drug 'im outer ther boozer:** the police dragged him out of the public house.

dry sod: A person deemed to have a subtle sense of humour. Conversely, a crashing bore is a **wet sod.**

dubs: A lavatory. **'e luvs 'is dubs:** he goes frequently to the lavatory.
Derived from "double-u-c".

ducks: Term of affection applied ironically to the opposite sex. Rarer than **luv** or **chooks.**

duck's disease: Condition attributed to a person who is long in the trunk and short in the legs. See **bum-droops.**

duff: Defective. **Yer flogged me a duff kettle.**

dun up like a fo'penny rabbit: Well dressed.

dursent: Dare not. The protective invocation of the Scouser maiden is **naw, I dursent, me Mam sez I shouldn't oughter.**

dymins: Supposedly diamonds but possibly white sapphires, zircons or paste. **'e guv 'er a ring wit' dymins like heggs.**

dynamite: Any effective laxative.

E

ear-basher: One who talks too much; a garrulous person.

eat up afore ther rats get at it: Hurry up with your meal.

e-bloody-nuff: More than enough.

'e come out like a busted boil: He emerged hurriedly and in a bad temper.

'e'd ferget 'is arse if it wasn't riveted on: Said of an absent-minded person.

'e'd pinch ther pennies off a dead man's eyes: He is unscrupulous.

'e done a pudden in 'is kecks: He was badly frightened.

Other similar phrases are: "'e done a fast faint an' they guv 'im artificial perspiration"; "'e tole 'is beads so fast 'e got finger-burns"; "'e printed ther map of England on 'is shairt-tail".

egg-bound: Constipated. **Aw cheese, I bin egg-bound fer a week.**

egg-shell blond: bald.

'e got ther chanst of goin' ter collitch or takin' up a military career: Said of a young hooligan to whom a magistrate has given the choice of going to Borstal or joining the Army.

'e knows a few werds—'e's bin ter collitch: Said of a garrulous bore.

'e's pist on ther chips: He has sabotaged our plans. *"Chips": firewood.*

'e's shet over ther boom: Of a seaman who has served under sail.

Em Dee (M.D.): **The Mersey Docks and Harbour Board.** When this title is pronounced in full it is considered scintillating to add **an' liddle lamsey divey.**

'ere's 'is 'ed 'is arse is cummin: Here is the man with a stoop.

Erny: An undertaker. The name is a joke based on *"urn-y"*.

endless belt: A prostitute.

ennit smashin'?: Isn't it wonderful?

'ere yar, Ma. Eighteenpence—One an' Eight!: Street traders' confidence trick.

er: Of, are. As in **one er this an' one er that**.

'e's 'ad 'is last fart: He has died.

ever 'ad yer 'ole in China?: This jest on a chamber-pot is the chorus-line of a rude folk-song.

excuse ther jam-jar, wontcher?: When following the local custom of offering beer in a jam-jar, this polite apology is intended to show that despite the container the host is well-trained in the social graces.

F

Faith, 'Ope an' Charity: Names applied sardonically to any trio of friends.

Other names are "Pip, Squeak and Wilfrid"; "Freeman, 'ardy and Willis"; Shake-ther-bed, Make-ther-bed and Inter-bed-yer-go", etc., etc. The latter is derived from the Biblical trio of Shadrach & Co

fallies: Bananas.

The origin of this word is obscure; possibly it arose from some humorist's habit of referring to bananas as phallic symbols.

Fancy Dan: A dressy person; a sartorial show-off. **A Fancy Dan muzzy:** a narrow, close-clipped moustache.

fangs: Teeth, especially false teeth. **Whur's me fangs?:** Where have I put my dentures?

A Liverpudlian's description of Mr Ken Dodd's teeth: "Ee could eat a apple through chicking-nettin'."

fang farrier: a dentist.

fard! fard!: A street cry announcing firewood for sale.

fardin: A farthing. **I wooden give a dead fardin fer it:** It's completely worthless.

Farder Bunloaf: Name usually applied to the local Roman Catholic priest when his name is not known. *Also "Farder Flat'at".*

Farder Christmas: A reluctant husband or lover. *From the jingle, "Christmas comes but once a year". See also "Jump Sunday".*

feckless keckless judy: A girl who distributes her favours with splendid impartiality.
See "Kecks".

feelin' ther strain: Constipated.

fents: Left-over oddments of the textile industry, often used for making cheap dresses. **fent-man:** a trader in such oddments. **fents** can also mean a fence as in **ther corpy's put a fents aroun' ther gardings.**

finick: A fussy, particular kind of person. **I'm tellin' yer she's a rill finick:** she is a fusspot.
Derived from "finicky".

finny-addy: Finnan haddock. Said of a person who is disliked: **got a face like a stale finny-addy.**

fist-fulla fives, a: a punch.

flags: Paving stones.
Hence a phrase such as "they 'ad ther flags up" means a riot and not a celebration.

flippin' 'eck!: A pointless exclamation equivalent to the Southern **cor lumme!**

Flyblown Phyllis: A prostitute.

fly pies: Derisory name for Eccles cakes.
Cf. Flies' cemetery.

Fore 'n' Aft Fanny: A prostitute.

four-eyed sod: Derisory term for a person who wears spectacles.

four mokes an' a full belt: The peak of success, namely, a ride in a four-horse carriage after a heavy meal.

frilly lips: A meaningless term of abuse, as in **'ey you wit' ther frilly lips.** Other similar terms are **'ey you wit' ther tatty hur** (hair); **'ey you wit' ther chopped-up eyebrows; 'ey you wit' ther messy gob,** etc., etc.

F.U.2.: This is the reply sometimes given when authority asks a suspect to name the number of the car he is driving.

fudge: To spoil something; to make a mess of it. **Yer prop'ly fudged that job, didn'tcher?**: A frequent cry of children playing marbles or cherry-bobs is **no fudgin'**!

fugginell: an all-purpose expression to express surprise, anger, etc.

funeral sugar: Lump or cube sugar, usually displayed in a high-class container such as a clean glass ash-tray filched from a pub. Also called **burial sugar. She thinks she's posh, she allus serves funeral sugar. funeral suit** or **burial suit**: A best suit, usually of heavy material and drab in colour, kept for special occasions.

fur ter middlin' (fair to middling): A grudging admission that the speaker's only complaint is that he has nothing about which to complain.

furries: Fairies. **Does yer believe in furries? Aye, but not in fairy** (furry) **furries** (fairies).

The vexed question as to the "correct" Scouse pronunciation of "fair" and "fur" is best illustrated by a notice which Liverpool Corporation Passenger Transport displayed in their vehicles (and in all seriousness) during the fifties:
    TREAT US FAIRLY—TRAVEL EARLY.

G

gaffer: A boss, foreman, overseer or even the father of a family.

gansey: A jersey or turtle-necked sweater.
Originally a "Guernsey Jacket".

Gas 'n' Choke Company, Ther: The North-Western Gas Board.
Derived from the former "Liverpool Gas & Coke Company".

gate: A bicycle. **twin-gate:** A tandem bicycle.

gear, ther: Very good, excellent, splendid.

gegs, ther: Same as above. A perverted form of **ther gear.**

General Balzup: A mythical authoritarian held responsible for any disorganization, defeat or failure.

genius: Sardonic name applied to any person considered to be a half-wit; one who makes foolish suggestions or offers impracticable advice.

gerraway!: An expression of wonder or disbelief.

gerund grinder: A schoolmaster.

get'nywhur?: This is a stock male-to-male enquiry about one's amatory successes the night before. The invariable reply is upon boastful lines such as **'ad ter dial 999 ter get away from it,** etc., etc.

get done: To be beaten up in a fight.

getsolt: To catch or grab, as in **I'll tan yer if I getsolt o' yer.**

gets on me tits: Annoys me very much. Other similar expressions are: **gets on me bib; gets on me wick; sends me up ther bloody wall; drives me winnuck,** etc., etc.

get set: Somebody is coming—prepare to run. See **dowse it.**

get stuck: A term of abuse. Others are **get stuffed; get buried, get boxed,,** etc., etc.

gippo: Gravy. **bags of gippo:** Lots of gravy.

given away wid a pound of tea: Said of something considered tawdry and worthless such as a very cheap engagement-ring. Other similar expressions are: **given away wid a squirt of milk; found it in a fuggin cracker** (a Christmas cracker), etc., etc.

give over: Stop it.

gives me ther gallopin' jerks: Annoys me very much.

give the boy a coconut: Sarcastic approval of a foolish act or especially stupid remark. An alternative phrase is **give ther boy a cough-drop.**

give us a squirt, wack: Please pass me the vinegar-bottle.

This elegant request is often heard in Merseyside fish-and-chip shops.

glannies: Glass marbles.

glass snots: Driblets of greenish, opalescent glass that can be clipped to the nostrils, thus giving the wearer the appearance of having a running and unwiped nose. The expert user provides a sound-track of glutinous sniffs. This is great fun.

gnashers: False teeth. **I knocked 'is gnashers down ter 'is arse:** I punched him in the mouth. See **fangs.**

gnats' piss: Cider, near beer, weak tea or any drink

considered to be lacking in strength.

goana: Going to. **I'm goana bop that sod**: I'm going to punch that fellow.

gob-organ: A mouth-organ or harmonica.

gob-wad: A plug of chewing tobacco.

God's gift ter wimmin: A conceited male; one who continually preens himself.

God knows 'e done 'er wrong: This is a fair example of the Scouser habit of saying something quite different from what is meant. The accusation is not levelled at God but is against some **derty tyke** who has put a girl in the family way. It is invariably uttered in self-righteous tones suggesting that the speaker's own virtue is beyond question.

goes up wit' ther bloody blind: Said of a person considered so feeble that when he pulls a spring-blind he gets hauled up with it.

gogs or **goggles**: Spectacles. **snout-gogs**: Pince-nez.

go 'ard astern: To give up the argument; to admit defeat and beat a hasty retreat.

goin' ter 'ave me hur did: Going for a hair-do, or Urdu.

goin' ter ther dogs: Not, as might be thought, heading for disaster, but attending the greyhound-racing tracks.

golly: A wad of phlegm. To **stick a golly on** someone: to spit on him.

See also "yocker".

gong: A chamber-pot. To **bong ther gong:** accidentally to kick the chamber-pot. A **gong** is also a medal.

good-oh: A term of enthusiastic approval.

See "whizzo".

go on, give yer penny ter ther monkey: Derisory condemnation of an intended purchase considered wasteful or stupid.

go on witcher: I don't believe it; you are pulling my leg.

goolies: Testicles. An orthodox invitation to a fight is **'ow'd yer like a kick in ther goolies?**

goosed: Tired out, exhausted, also spoiled or messed up. As in **yer prop'ly goosed that job, didn'tcher?**

got a face like a dollop of mortal sins: Said of someone who is disliked or considered repulsive.
See "finny-addy". "Got a" is usually pronounced "Gorra".

got a gob like a bee's bum: Said of a sarcastic person; one given to making biting or stringing remarks.

got a neck like a mad giraffe: Said of a cheeky, impudent person.

got any jam-jars, missus?: The regular question of children earning pocket-money by collecting empty jars.

got a well-stuffed mattress: Said of a penny-pincher, a miserly person. Another phrase: **got a long stockin' somewhur.**

got bored: Sardonic comment on a mother-to-be, especially one regarded as getting on in years.

go ter bits: To collapse in a figurative sense; to throw up the sponge.

got it stamped on 'is arse: Said of a persistent drunkard, the cogent word being **beer.**

got married at St. Paul's: Said of a girl believed to have surrendered her virginity. The reference is to

St. Paul's Square, Liverpool.

got more kid than a pregnant goat: Said of a leg-puller; an incurable joker.

got more bum than brains: Said of a simpleton.

got piles like seaweed: Said of a restless, fidgety person.

got rabies: Said of a foul-tempered, quarrelsome person.

gotta tur in me kecks: I have a tear in my trousers.

got ther gob-shakes: Said of a persistent talker, especially a nagging woman.

got ther luck of soft Joe: Very lucky indeed.

got tin tits an' an iron arse: Said of a large, formidable, well-corseted woman.

gowfer: A golfer; one who plays with **gowf-clubs.**

gozzie: A contraceptive named, for reasons not made clear, "Gossamer".

grad: A person who has been to a reform school or a

Borstal institution. A graduate.

graft: Tedious or tiring work. **I don't like this 'ere job—it's too much 'ard graft.**

grasser: A police informant; a stool-pigeon.

Grid, Ther: The railway sidings and marshalling yards at Bankhall, Liverpool.

griff: News; information.
Also "griffin".

grind: Sexual intercourse. "The daily grind and common task" therefore has a special meaning to Scousers. The past tense is **grund**.
But in Irish parlance "grind" is still used in the 19th-century English sense, meaning studying hard, with a tutor, for an examination; or "cramming". Advertisements frequently appear in Irish papers soliciting, for example, "English grind, twice weekly . . ." and cause some puzzlement to visitors. See "Gerund Grinder".

grizzle like an oven-tap: To complain or whine, feebly but persistently.
The reference is to a small-bore brass tap attached to the hot-water tank in the old-fashioned fireplace cooking range. Such taps often dripped for hours.

grope: To attempt the preliminaries to a seduction.

grotty: Grotesque, ugly.

gruesome twosome: An ill-assorted couple.

gummy bastard: An elderly person, especially one who does not **wur 'is gnashers** (wear his false teeth).

gurgle: A woman's girdle. **I laffed so 'ard I bust me gurgle.**

guv: The past tense of give. As in **I guv 'im a kick in ther moosh** (mouth).

'alf seas over: Drunk, especially when lurching or staggering. Other phrases are **'alf cut; 'alf soaked; 'alf pissed: 'alf shot,** etc., etc.

'am 'n' Egg Parade, Ther: Victoria Road, New Brighton.
Derived from the number of restaurants in this road.

'appy as a dog wit' two dicks: Very happy indeed.

'ard crap: Bad luck. Also **'ard cheese,** or **'ard cheddar.**

'ard knock: A tough case.

'ard skin: A person who is very tough, usually in his own estimation.

'arry Petty's: An old and well-known Liverpool restaurant that long specialised in providing cheap meals for office boys and junior clerks.
"Does yers all want heggs, does yers?" used to be the server's rhetorical question.

'ave a wack: To make an attempt; to have a go.

'ave ther shutters off, to: A street brawl in which shutters are torn from shop windows and used as weapons.

'e spewed 'is ring up: He vomited.

'ead serang: A boss or foreman.
This is a shipping term arising from the employment of Asiatic crews, especially lascars or natives of the Coromandel Coast of India.

'iggerant: Bad mannered, uncouth, ignorant. **I jes' can't stan' that feller, 'e's plain bloody 'iggerant.**

'og jockey: A term of abuse.

'olesaler: A brothel keeper.

'oly Joe: A person who is prim and proper; one who advertises his piety; a lay preacher.

'oo Flung Dung: Name given to Chinese persons whose real names are not known or have been forgotten.
Despite the crudity, the purpose is jocular and no insult is intended. The Chinese enjoy fair popularity on Merseyside and their restaurants are nationally renowned.

'ooley: A dispute, a fight or a riot.

'ot kecks: Amorous. **She's got 'ot kecks fer 'im:** she fancies that man.

'uffy: Annoyed. As in **I tole 'er ther rill fax an' she got proper 'uffy.**

'ummer: A children's toy made from a perforated can-lid and a loop of string. **'e's playin' wit' 'is 'ummer** implies that the adult referred to is senile. Another type of **'ummer** consists of a wood lath whirled around at the end of a piece of string; the Australian **bull-roarer.**

'ur: Hair. **She's got rilly fur 'ur:** she has really fair hair.

I

I ain't goin' ter tur me 'ur over 'air: I'm not going to tear my hair over her.

Ickey, ther firebobby: The fireman.

I could do yer in me sleep: Retort given to an aggressive arguer or to someone spoiling for a fight. Other phrases are **I could do yer wit' one 'and tied behind me back; I could lay yer out in five seconds flat; if I blew me nose yer'd fall over,** etc., etc.

I didn' cum over wit' me 'ed stickin' out uv a crate: I am not an Irish immigrant.

if I'd known yez was comin' I'd 'ave brung me ortergraff book: Derisory welcome calculated to deflate the visitor on arrival.

if yer don't look out yer'll get washed all over: This sinister threat refers to the practice of washing a corpse before burial.

if yer kilts yerself I'll bloody well merder yer: Orthodox warning to a Scouser child concerning the wrath to come.

I'll tell on yer: I will betray you.

I'm stuck wit' me gorilla: This alarming piece of information from a Scouser housewife usually results in a fitter being sent to repair her gas cooker grill.
This is an example of the intrusive vowel sounds often heard in the Irish dialects—"fillum" for "film" and even "bering" for "bring", etc.

'im with ther Cunard feet: The man with big splay feet.

'im: My husband.

I'm walkin' on ther blackin': My shoes need repairing.

I remember when 'is arse wuz outa 'is kecks: I knew him before he was prosperous.

'i-SKRIM: A musical street cry meaning ice-cream for sale. Now largely replaced by unmusical chimes fitted to ice-cream vans—the modern pied pipers which each year lure scores of children to their deaths in road accidents.

It: Sexual intercourse.

The following true incident is reported by a young eye-witness from a French lesson at a well-known Liverpool girls' grammar school.

Senior mistress: "We will translate into French: I—am—thinking—about—him." (Giggles from the class.)

"Very well, if you think that's so funny I will change it. I—am—thinking—about—It." (Collapse of discipline.)

Island, Ther: The Isle of Man.

'is Mam's got a rice pudden in ther oven fer 'im: Jeering comment on a person regarded as a weakling.

issue, ther: The complete job, the lot. **Yer've buggered up ther 'ole issue:** you've made a total mess of it.

it broke off in a 'ard frost: Snide comment on a determined bachelor.

Not to be confused, however, with "She broke it off", which refers to an engagement or close friendship.

itchy powder: Lice.

A euphemism derived from an irritant powder sold by joke shops.

it's in ther bag: It is settled, arranged.

"It's in the pipeline" means much the same thing when used as a convenient cliché by politicians or industrialists—especially when promising a pay award—in the comforting knowledge of not having to divulge the length of the pipe.

it's me back: This is a standard excuse for avoiding work wherever possible. **Me doctor sez I can't do nuttin but light wairk—it's me back.**

it's sky-blue pink wit' a finny-addy border: Said of something regarded as having everything, such as an imposing mansion or a Rolls Royce car.

it's ther rich what 'as ther pleasures; it's ther poower what gets ther blame: Misquotation of cockney song sometimes sung in moments of stress.

I want ter carry ther banner: Jeering comment on a person who whines that his merits are unappreciated.

J

jack: A detective. **sly-jack:** A shop or store detective.

"As keen as two jacks in a petty": Very sharp-witted. In this phrase "petty" is a reference to sneak-thieves who rob lavatory-locks.

jangler: A piano.

jangler-wangler: A pianist or a teacher of the piano.

jangling: gossiping.

jannock: The real truth. **I'm tellin' yer an' that's jannock:** I am telling the absolute truth. The origin of this strange word is not known.

"jannock" = *genuine, straight-forward.*

jar: Half a pint. **jar of ale:** A half-pint of beer. A **few** jars usually means a good many as in **aye, I've 'ad a few jars,** meaning more than enough.

jes binter: Just been to. **I jes binter ther clinic an' they sez I'm on ther way agin.**

Jesus boots: sandals.

Jesus Fluid: holy water.

Derived from the well-known disinfectant, Jeyes Fluid.

Jester: The City of Chester. **We bin a trip ter ther Jester Zoo.**

jigger: A back alley.

jigger-jerker: One who has or claims to have frequent amorous adventures in back alleys.

jimmy riddle, to have a: To urinate. Said of a person with a weak bladder: **'e's got ther jimmy riddles.**

Rhyming slang with "piddle". Cockney importation.

jink: A Jonah, a bringer of bad luck.

Back-formation from "jinx", on the assumption that this word is plural, like Chinese.

Jinny Greenteeth: The ghost of a child-eating female said to haunt St. James's Cemetery.

jirry or **jerry:** A chamber-pot.

jocks: Testicles.

Joe Soap: Whozit, whatzisname. When asked by the police to account for the possession of a stolen article the answer often is **I got guv it by Joe Soap.**

John Peel: One who boasts of his amatory successes. *The reference is to peel in the sense of undressing.*

join the mounties, to: To have sexual intercourse.

jollop: Medicine, especially a liquid laxative. **If yer don't wallop yer jollop yer'll get ther beezers in yer belly.**

jowler: A back alley.

jowler-yowler: An alley cat.

judy: A girl or young woman. A favourite excuse when caught loitering with intent to commit a felony is **I were waitin' fer me judy.** The police check on this by waiting for the **judy** themselves, usually in vain.

jug: A pint. **jug of ale:** A pint of beer.

jumbo: Large, very big. **A jumbo job:** A very big task.

Jump Sunday: A Sunday prior to the Grand National Horse-race during which the public tours the course at Aintree and inspects the jumps. Hence said of a reluctant lover or inadequate husband: **'e saves it fer Jump Sunday.**

jump-up: A person envied for having made progress; one thought of as having gained undeserved promotion.

K

Kairky: The Liverpool district of Kirkdale. Not to be confused with the new township of Kirkby, pronounced **Kairby.**

kay-fisted: Left-handed.

kavley: A sing-song, or musical get-together.
Cf. Irish word "Ceilidh", meaning the same. "Kaylied" means drunk.

kecks: Drawers, panties, shorts or trousers.

keepin' dem on ther run: Scratching one's head or armpits.
dem = vermin.

keepin' it in ther family: Incest.
The BBC is probably still blissfully unaware of the amusement it caused in Liverpool when naming one of their programmes "Two-way Family Favourites".

keep it in yer nut: Treat it confidentially, keep it to yourself.

keep yer thievin' 'ands off me barrer: This is the long-established shout of Merseyside street traders.

kewins: Winkles.

kick-ther-can: A form of street football, using old tin cans.

kick ther cat: To show a petulant display of temper and vent one's ire upon an innocent party.

kidspector: An inspector of the R.S.P.C.C.

kilt: Past tense of kill.

King Kong: Derisory name for a weedy, undersized individual.
Cf. "Tiny" for a very tall man.

king o' ther midden: A conceited person; one who puts on airs.

Klondike: The Orrell district of Bootle. This odd name was acquired at the time when the digging of a large clay-pit for brickmaking coincided with the opening of a nearby tin-smelting works.

knacker's yard: Said of a place that looks a complete mess.

knee-bender: A pious person.

knees up, Mother Brown: This is sometimes shouted after an **owd biddy** (elderly woman) when she is the worse for drink.

knife 'n' fork tea: A substantial early-evening meal, or a meal in which the host has included some kind of meat.

knocked rotten: To be knocked silly; to be beaten into a stupor.

knocking shop: A brothel.

knucks: A brass knuckleduster or anything used in lieu, such as a piece of chain wrapped around the fist.

L

Lady Muck of Muck Hall: A woman who puts on airs, has a condescending manner and is regarded as excessively conceited. Less often called **Lady de Blobswitch.**

last back-end: The latter part of the previous year.

Last Supper, Ther: Sardonic name for fish and chips.

leave it open, wack: A public lavatory plea exemplifying the old adage "Take care of the pennies and the pounds will take care of themselves."

lecky: Electricity. Formerly also used for Liverpool trams, i.e. Electric Cars.

lemmings: Not mysterious migrants from Norway but lemons. These are hawked in Liverpool to the very old cry of **four fer a shillun them fine lemmings** —or whatever the current price might be.

lemme be: Leave me alone. When a Scouser is caught misbehaving his usual whine to the police officer is

why don'tcher lemme be? An alternative protest is **aw cheese, hen't yer got nuttin better ter do?**

lenusser meg: Can I borrow some money? **I'm skint, lenusser meg.**

lett'ns: A Corporation housing department.
From "lettings", i.e. an office where living accommodation is let.

lezzy: A lesbian woman.

Lice Palace, Ther: The Lyceum Theatre, Liverpool. Also called the **Old Licey**.

like a bitch on heat: Worried, restless, fidgety.

like two apples in a bag: Description of a girl's back view.

lissen ter 'er wit' ther gob: Derisory dismissal of another woman's argument or complaint.

locust beans: Carob beans used in the manufacture of cattle-food. Considered a delicacy by children.

locust kernels: The hard seeds of carob beans used to produce a very fine flour as a base for certain cosmetics.

long string o' misery: A person who whines; a perpetual complainer.

long string o' summat-er-other: Said of a person who is disliked.

Lord Muck of Muck Hall: A bombastic person; a swollen-headed man who likes to assert his authority.

lost 'is marbles: Said of a bewildered, muddle-minded person.

Luke Har: A person regarded as having a precious accent; one who speaks with strained correctness and in a condescending manner.

Probably derived from the derisory phrase "oh, ay say, luke har!"

lurk or **lerk:** A job, occupation, especially a racket or paying hobby. **What's yer lerk?:** what do you do to make money?

A mispronunciation of the Cockney "lark".

luv: Ironical term of affection applied to the opposite sex. Often used by waitresses as in **what'll yer 'ave luv?** to which the stock answer is **what yer willin' ter give me?** Also by bus conductoresses as in **'ow far jer wanter go, luv?** to which the standard counter is **'ow far will yer let me?** and the riposte

Ile tell yer where ter get off.

Scousers are very fond of accusing non-Scouser comedians of stealing this kind of repartee, but in fact it is even more expertly practised in the U.S.A.

M

mad as Barney's bull: Very angry.

made-up: Happy, pleased.

Mairsy dopes an' dozey dopes: Derisory name for Merseyside.

make 'im frow up: Suggested cure for a stomachache or a bilious feeling, especially when the sufferer is a child. This advice may be accompanied by the further suggestion of **stick yer finger down 'is froat.**

manna from hevving: Bird droppings, especially those of seagulls.

mard: Spoilt. **mard kid:** Spoilt child.
Probably from "marred".

mardy: Petulant, whining. **She's got a rill mardy kid.**

Marshy Musketeers, Ther: The Salvation Army,

specifically in Bootle where their Citadel stood adjacent to Marsh Lane.

matchie: An employee of *Bryant & May's* match-works.

In the Classified Directory, Liverpool's yellow pages, this firm is entered under "Match Makers".

matinee, 'avin. a: Daytime sexual intercourse.

me belly thinks me froat's cut: I am very hungry.

medsin: Medicine. Also applied to spirits such as whisky or gin.

meg: A halfpenny. See **red meg**.

me Mam: My mother, as in **whur's me Mam?**

me marrer run colt: I was shocked, scared, badly frightened.

merry: This means its precise opposite, namely, foul-tempered, quarrelsome. A regular excuse for assaulting a police officer is **I'd 'ad a few gills** (of beer) **an' got a bit merry.**

Mersey Funnel, The: A general nickname for the new Roman Catholic cathedral, Liverpool, which is funnel, or tent-shaped. Also **Paddy's Wigwam**.

So far as we know, no-one has yet remarked on the resemblance the lantern of this new cathedral bears to the upper part of the tower of St. Peter's Church—a beautiful edifice erected in 1700 that once stood in Church Street, on the present site of Woolworths. It was demolished in 1922—sacrificed on the altar of commerce by the Church Commissioners of the time, to their everlasting shame.

"*Then I saw there was a way to hell,*
Even from the gates of Heaven."
(John Bunyan : "The Pilgrim's Progress)

message: An errand. **I'm doin' a message fer an owd doll**: I'm going an errand for an old lady.

mess up 'is moosh: To express disagreement by breaking a glass or a bottle and jabbing the ragged end into the other person's face.

mess up 'is wedd'n': To kick an opponent in the lower part of the body.

Another threat is "I'll plan yer family!"

meter inspector: Sardonic name for a sneak-thief who tries to gain entrance to houses by pretending that he is an official sent to read the meters.

Met, Ther: The Metropole Theatre, Bootle, now demolished.

Mick: An Irishman. **As mad as a Mick in ther nick:** as annoyed as an Irishman in jail.

mickey: A pigeon. **mickey-snatcher:** A person who steals municipal pigeons.

Micky Drippin': Whozit, Whatzisname?

milkie: A milkman. Said of a flirtatious housewife: **she keeps ther milkie on ther doorstep fer ars** (hours).

mince: Minutes. As in **see yer in a coupler mince.**

mind yer car, mister?: The war-cry of a juvenile protection racket operating on many unattended parking lots round theatres, football grounds, etc. The implication is—pay up now or else find your car damaged when you return.

mind yer own 'indrance: Mind your own business. An alternative phrase is **mind yer own sufrance** (sufferance).

mingy: Mean, penny-pinching. **Mingy-arsed bastard:** a miserly person.

misery moo: A teetotaler: a person who prefers soft drinks, especially milk.

mizzle: To flee or disappear, usually to avoid the police.

moan: To complain, to grumble. **moanin' on ther bar:** To seek sympathy from a bartender; to weep into one's beer.

Perhaps a punning reference to fog warnings near The Bar sandbanks.

mo-bike: A motorcycle.

Moby Dick: A nude male statue by Jacob Epstein much admired for its generous proportions. Located over the entrance of Lewis's Ltd. in the centre of Liverpool.

Cf. Liverpool folk-joke: First Welsh Lady to Second Welsh Lady (both shopping in Liverpool on Thursday afternoon): "What's that?" 2nd W.L.: "That's Lewises." 1st W.L.: "It looks more like Owen Owen's."

moggie: A cat. **top-moggie:** A tomcat. **jigger-rabbit:** Stray cat.

Cf. "moghe": Gaelic for small, dainty.

moke: Any kind of equine quadruped from a seaside donkey to a one-ton carthorse.

Moke Street: Lightbody Street, Liverpool, in bygone days replete with carthorses.

molar-mauler: A dentist.

money fer owd rope: Something for nothing. Other similar phrases are **money fer dirt; money fer raggety kecks; money fer jam,** etc., etc.

Money Street: A street in Liverpool properly called **The Old Ropery.**

monkey 'ouse: A monastery; also the Council Chamber.

moo: Milk. **stiff-moo:** Condensed milk. See **conny-**

mook-cart (muck-cart): A refuse truck. Said of a despised family **when they was shiftin'** (moving house) **they called in ther mook-cart.**

mook in: Help yourself. **mook in, yer at yer granny's:** Grab a share of whatever is available.

moonlight flit, to do a: To move one's furniture and household possessions to another address, in the middle of the night, the purpose being to evade the landlord and other creditors.

moony: Absent-minded, dreamy, romantic.

moosh: The lower portion of the face, around the

mouth. **'ey you wit' ther maggerty moosh.**

mop: To drink, especially beer. Many a Scouser considers it flattering to be known as **a bloody good booze-mopper.**

mortal sin: Any form of pleasure. **'ad a good time on me 'olidays—I done a few mortal sins.**

Moses: A garrulous old man. **'e yaps like Moses readin' ther bloody tablets.**

mother superior: Any kind of female boss; a forewoman, overseer, supervisor or matron. Also called a **tawny owl, Auntie Muriel, Mrs. Macnamara** (the leader of the band), etc., etc.

Mother's Milk: Guinness, a popular brand of stout.

mouse-'ole, Ther: A two-lane, second "bottle-neck" road tunnel under the Mersey begun in 1964. Like the Runcorn-Widnes bridge it was already too small while still on the drawing board.

mouse-turd: Mustard.

mug: To buy or pay for. **mug yer a jar of ale:** I'll buy you a glass of beer. **oo's muggin'?** Who is paying this time?

Mur, Ther: The Mayor. **After ther Lord Mur's Show comes ther mook-cart.**

There was an incident on Merseyside not many years ago when by coincidence a royal procession was immediately preceded along the crowd-lined route by a Corporation dustcart. One of the dustmen, wearing the traditional broad-brimmed hat, and seated in a dustbin so far forgot himself as to mimick the characteristic, diffident, hand-wave of royalty. It is a measure of the British sense of fair play, freedom of expression and—not least—humour, that it was not only the crowd that hugely enjoyed the joke. Following the by no means inevitable summons for insulting behaviour there was a request from the royal person concerned that there should be no prosecution. All this could only happen in England.

Mury Helen (Mary Ellen): A working-class Liverpool woman, usually elderly and of scruffy appearance. Once known as a **shawlie** from the Irish habit of wearing a shawl. Less frequently called a **Mury Han (Mary Ann)**.

mush: A neutral form of address less used than **wack**.

muster bin: Must have been. **I don't remember nuttin about it, I muster bin bevvied.**

mutton dagger: penis.

muzzied: Muddle-minded, witless, usually through drink.

muzzy: A moustache. **a muzzy like two snots:** A narrow, close-clipped moustache. See **Fancy Dan.**

N

nance: An effeminate male. Also called a **nancy, queenie, one er them, ship's Mary,** etc., etc.

nark: A dispute, a quarrel.

narky: Irritable, bad-tempered. As in **I've 'ad e-bloody-nuff er you gettin' narky over nuttin.**

Nash, Ther: The Grand National horse-race. **'ave a bash at ther Nash:** To make a bet on the race. **Ther Nash** can also mean the **National Assistance Board,** as in **she dunned a coupler bob from ther Nash.** Also **Nab,** or **N.A.B.**

natter: To gossip or talk. Also to lecture or give lengthy reproof. To nag at someone. **owd natterbag:** a scolding woman.

N.B.: New Brighton, a district of the borough of Wallasey.

Netherfield Road Navy: The bands of the **Loyal Order of Orange Lodges,** usually dressed in quasi-naval uniforms.

nickers: Cigarette butts.

Derived from the habit of nicking (pinching) a cigarette to put it out and keeping it for future use.

niggle: to question; to raise objections.

nit: A silly person. A fool. As in **wotcher do that fer, yer daft nit?**

nits: Lice or the eggs of lice. **me 'ur's fuller nits**: my hair is infested with lice. See **biddies.**

nix: Nothing. **got it fer nix**: Obtained it for nothing. **keepin' nix**: Keeping watch to see that nothing interferes with some illegal or immoral activity.

From German "nichts", nothing.

ni-sharp!: A street cry meaning knives sharpened.

nobbut: Nothing but.

nonk: A large clay marble.

Norshore, Ther: The North Shore Flour Mills, Ltd.

nowse: Skill, flair, knowledge.

From the Greek "noûs" (itself a contraction of "noos", meaning "mind"). One of the strangest survivals in dialect usage of a word long obsolete (perhaps it was too "noetic"— same root!) in normal speech.

nowt: Nothing. As in **I'm 'avin' nowt ter do wit' it.**
"Nowt" is interchangeable with "nix" and "nuttin" and used about as frequently.

nut: Head. To **put in ther nut:** To butt someone with one's head.

nut-pox: Ringworm.

nuts: Testicles. **I've cracked me nuts:** I am in great pain.

O

of: Have. **I could of:** I could have.

O.K. but don't drag me past me muvver's: A female's mock-reluctant consent to her importuning lover.
The reference is to the canine lack of reticence when engaged in amatory pursuits.

old school tie: A hangman's noose.

oldest railway in ther world: Jocularly said of the railway system in the Wirral Peninsula, alluding to the Biblical statement that God made all creeping things.

ollies: Marbles or the game of marbles. A mispronunciation of **alleys.**

once round Maggie, twice round ther gasworks: Said of a very stout woman.

one er Lewis's: A wax dummy. **don't stand there like one er Lewis's:** Don't pose like a wax dummy.
The reference is to Lewis's departmental store.

Onion: Name sometimes given to a Welshman, especially one called **Einion.**

on ther game: Engaged in prostitution.

on ther job: Engaged in sexual intercourse.

on ther pig's back: Lucky; doing well; in the money.

on ther piss: Drinking with the sole intention of getting drunk rather than for company and good cheer.

on ther ropes: In trouble.

oodles: Lots of. **Oodles of woo:** Lots of sexual intercourse.

oojah-capiff: A whatzit, a thingumebob. **Whur's ther oojah-capiff?:** Where is the hammer, spanner or whatever it might be?

organ-grinder: A person who brags of his bedroom exploits; a self-styled sexual athlete.

orilly thasso?: An expression of polite indifference with a suggestion of disbelief.

outer wairk: Unemployed.

'ow about er bit?: A mating call usually uttered with (real or simulated) hoarse passion in back alleys.

owd: Old. **Owd geezer:** An elderly man. **Owd nit:** An old and slovenly woman.

owd oil: A persuasive but untrue story usually uttered in a whining tone. **I guv 'im ther owd oil:** I tried to cajole him. A less-used American importation is **razzmatazz,** as in **I guv 'im ther razzmatazz.**

P

Paddy's Market: A Liverpool market well-known for the sale of second-, third- or fourth-hand clothing.

paddywack: An indigestible ligament of meat, used by children as something upon which to chew.

From it probably arises a folk-song with the chorus "knick-knack paddywack, give a dog a bone", etc., etc.

pairce: A purse. **That ther bloody woming jes' swiped me pairce!** is an accusation shrieked from time to time in Merseyside stores. Said of a skinflint **'e turns 'is back on yer when 'e looks inter 'is pairce.**

pairks: A rake-off or percentage, usually confiscated without knowledge or permission.

See also "bunce".

pairm: A hair-do; a permanent wave. As in **'ey, look at 'er wit' ther potty pairm.**

Pantown: The township of *Moreton,* now big and

modern, but once known for its large number of caravans, shanties and tents.

A Scouser story then current told that a "floater" (dead body) had been fished out of the Mersey and identified as an inhabitant of Moreton by the bucket-ring on its backside. Also called "Bucketville".

par: Power. As in **'e wairks at ther par-station.**

passin'-out p'rade: An assembly of relatives at the bedside of a sick and possibly dying person.

penguin-'ouse: A nunnery.

Penny Bridge: A bridge across the northern end of the Cheshire dock system linking Birkenhead with Wallasey.

Penny Road Bridge: A bridge across the Leeds and Liverpool canal leading from Pennington Road, Litherland.

pennuth o' God 'elp us: Description of a person considered trivial and insignificant.

perve: Any man who openly admires girls.

petty: A lavatory. **petty-pirate**: A lavatory attendant. **petty-poet**: One who expresses his soul-stirrings upon lavatory walls, a graffitist.

piecer: A portion or share. As in **I guv 'im a piecer me mind.**

piles: Lots of. As in **that feller's got piles er money.**

pill: A cigarette.

pine chips: A popular meal consisting of meat pie and fried potatoes.

pinky: A small clay marble.

pinny-full: A pinafore full; a lot. Said of a woman considered of loose morals: **she comes 'ome wit' a pinny-full er tuppences.** Said of a woman visibly pregnant: **'e guv 'er a pinny-full all right.**

piss along like a green goddess, to: To move very fast. The reference is to a speedy and comfortable type of tram or street-car known locally as **a green goddess,** now replaced by buses and, some think, more's the pity.

piss-prophet: A Physician.

Derived from the age-old practice of diagnosing illness by examining the patient's urine.

Pisseries, Ther: The Stoke-on-Trent area. Derived

from **The Potteries,** and the sanitary ware made there.

playin' put 'n' take: Sexual intercourse.

p.o.: Not a post-office but a probation officer. **'e's under 'is p.o.**: He is in the care of a probation officer.

pobs: Bread and hot milk or any insipid meal similar thereto. The phrase **go 'ome to yer pobs!** implies that the person so addressed is either a baby or senile.

pole-squatter: A prostitute.

pong: A smell. **a dairty great pong**: A very bad smell.

ponko: An old shawl or worn-out blanket. **'e** (the pawnbroker) **wooden give a tanner on me ponko.** *Derived from "poncho".*

poop-pusher: A laxative, especially one of satisfactory violence.

pot: A chamber-pot. **potty** or **totty-pot**: A child's chamber-pot. A **pot** is also a carburettor. To **tickle ther pot**: To prime a carburettor.

potcheen (potheen): Any pain-killing liquor from methylated spirits to paint-stripper.

Pox Palace, Ther: The famous **Liverpool Museum of Anatomy** which, among other things, displayed models demonstrating the evils of venereal disease. The building was bombed during the last war.

pozzy: Jam or any preserve, especially the tinned variety, issued to the armed forces.

Veterans of the 1914-18 war remember getting issues of a brand of condensed milk called "Posy Brand" while in the trenches.

Preston Guild: A municipal celebration held in Preston, Lancashire, every twenty years.

Hence "once every Preston Guild" is an expression equivalent to "once in a blue moon", i.e., very seldom.

Pricey buckos: Derisory name given by **Brutal scruffs** to youths living in the Price Street area of Birkenhead.

prick-teaser: A girl who leads her man on but who refuses to be seduced.

prod pairmit: A marriage certificate.

proper: Real, really. **proper champion:** Really good.

Prot or **Protisant:** A Protestant. **Prot parade:** the annual parade of the **Loyal Order of Orange**

Lodges. Also **Proddy-dog.**

> *Cf. Liverpool children's rhyme:*
> *Proddy-dog, Proddy-dog, sitt'n on a well;*
> *Up came ther devil an' pulled 'im down ter 'ell.*

prurs: Prayers. **Chwistopher Wobin is saying 'is prurs** is a taunt flung at a clean, fussily-dressed child, usually before kicking him in the buttocks.

Pudden Club, Ther: The condition of pregnancy. **she's joined ther Pudden Club:** She has become pregnant. Or simply **Ther Club.**

pudden pickin': Living on immoral earnings.

pull ther lanyard, to: To pass wind loudly.

Nautical: from the method of sounding the audible warnings on ships.

pull up ther ladder: I couldn't care less; I am indifferent. This is a shortened version of the naval saying **pull up the ladder, Jack—I'm in the dinghy.**

pullet-squeezer: A man with a fondness for young girls, or for virgins.

pusher: A mock-auctioneer's accomplice.

put a crust on ther Rosy fer 'im: He has a good appetite.

Rosy : a ship's swill bin.

put it on ther slate: Debit me with it.
Queen Anne front an' Mury Ann back: Said of a
put it whur ther monkey puts ther nuts! A polite alternative for a more common answer often given to questioners who ask "Where shall I put it?"

put on ther dog: To show off; to make oneself the centre of attention.

puts 'is foot in ther pot an' pees down 'is trouser leg: Said of a very shy, self-conscious person.

put ther boot in: To kick a fallen opponent in the head, ribs or abdomen.

put ther nut in: To seize a person by the coat-lapels and butt him in the face.

put ther thumbs in: To try to gouge out an opponent's eyes.

Q

Queen Anne front an' Mury Ann back: Said of a woman considered uppish and a cut or two above her neighbours. Also said of a house thought to be all show with nothing behind it.

queenie: An effeminate male.

queen o' ther midden: A conceited woman; a show-off.

queen o' ther wash-house: An authoritative gossip; a persistent scandal-monger.

queer (or quare) feller, ther: Whozit, whatsizname. **whur's ther queer feller?** Where is the boss or foreman whose name I don't know?

quick drag: A few hasty puffs on a cigarette, usually in forbidden circumstances.
Persons accustomed to clandestine smoking can always be recognised by the manner in which they hold their cigarettes (even when smoking openly), i.e. between forefinger and thumb, the lighted end shielded by the palm.

R

raddips: Rabbits. **I ast me butcher fer a fresh raddip but 'e 'adn't got none.**

raddled: Bewildered, confused. A mispronunciation of **rattled**.

raggety kecks: Worn-out knickers or tattered drawers. **'ey, look at 'er wit' ther raggety kecks** implies that the person referred to is a slummy.

rags: Any form of clothing. **funeral rags**: Best clothes.

randy sod: An amorous person; a lady-killer.
As in "E's randy like a butcher's dog".

rat catchers: R.Cs. Roman Catholics.

rattler: A tram or street-car, or (plural) the stairs thereof, or any stairs.

red biddy: Very cheap harsh wine, sometimes mixed with stout and spiked with gin.

red-blooded all-American fullback: Derisory term for a braggart; a self-styled hero.

Red Hot John: A Salvation Army officer in Bootle, well known for his reformist zeal. Said of an angry wife ticking off an errant husband **she guv 'im 'ell, like Red Hot John.**

red meg: A mythical coin of no value whatever. **it ain't worth a red meg:** It is completely worthless.

Redneck: A Catholic.
Also "Cogger" or "Left-footer" or "Ail Mury", "Rat Catcher" or "Crate Egg"

red raddle: A hard block of red powder used for cleaning and colouring window-sills, doorsteps and brickwork.

remember ther Boyne!: War-cry of the Orangemen, less heard in present times.

Respice, Aspice, Prospice, All-pis: The civic motto of Bootle as adapted by the more cynical of its inhabitants.

Rhubarb Vaselino: Rudolph Valentino. Said of a youthful preener who considers himself **ther gear: 'oo does 'e think 'e is, Rhubarb Vaselino?**

rill fax: The naked truth. As in **I guv 'im ther rill fax an' 'e went inter a tizzy.**

ring ther bell: To make a woman pregnant. Said of the father of a large family **'e rings ther bell ev'ry time. ring ther bell!** is also a cry once screamed by children when other children were stealing rides on the rear bumpers of street-cars. See **whip behind.**

rip: To pass wind with unseemly vigour.
Hence Scousers find Jack the Ripper somewhat amusing.

Rock, Ther: Perch Rock Battery: New Brighton. Also Gibraltar. Also the dance.

roller or **roll-boy:** A very pious person.
Possibly derived from: "When the roll is called up yonder I'll be there.

rollin' in ther shit: Thoroughly drunk.

ropey: Bad; of poor quality. **a ropey do:** A disappointing affair.

Rose Garden, Ther: Linacre Road Gasworks, Bootle.

Rose of Tralee: Sardonic name given to an old and slovenly woman.

rotten: Very drunk.

rozzer: A police constable. See **scuffer** and **slop**.

rubbidge: Rubbish. A common way of dismissing an argument is to say **thasser lotter rubbidge**.

rube: A fairground or circus attendant.

runs: Diarrhoea. **go like a bookie wit' ther runs:** To move very fast.

Ruthless Rufus: Whozit, whatsizname, applied specifically to a person in a position to administer punishment, such as a headmaster or a magistrate.

S

saddy: Cruel. Derived from **sadistic.**

sag: To absent oneself. To **play sag:** To play truant from school, or just **saggin' skewl.**

sage-er-mint-er-parsley!: A very old street cry shouted by female vendors, mostly outside St. John's Market, Liverpool.

Sally Gash: The Salvation Army.

sandgrounders or **sandgrubbers:** Citizens of Southport.

Not to be confused with "sandgropers" who are inhabitants of Western Australia.

sanny: A sanitary inspector. As in **we've 'ad ther sanny round ter find ther pong.**

sass: Sarsaparilla, a soft drink.

sawdust's cummin outa me knees, The: I am exhausted, very tired.

savoury ducks: Faggots.

scadge: To beg or borrow. Composite of **scrounge** and **cadge**.

scoff: Food. As in **whur's me scoff?:** Where is my food?.

scoots: Roller-skates. It can also mean diarrhoea as in **cheese, I fur got ther scoots.**

scouse: From the Norwegian **Labskaus:** a cheap and easily prepared type of stew for which there are numerous recipes. **dead-scouse:** The same stew when cold. **blind-scouse:** A cheap stew made without meat. **Scouse** is also the name given to the Merseyside dialect.
(See "Lern Yerself Scouse" for a fuller explanation.)

Scouser: An inhabitant of Merseyside, not necessarily a Liverpudlian. This book assumes a narrower definition, namely, a Merseysider who speaks **Scouse**.

screw: A prison officer. **screwdriver:** A prison governor. **screw** can also mean to commit a burglary or to have sexual intercourse, or wages.
Hence "a bloody good screw" might refer to an attractive girl or to a place considered suitable for a robbery, or a good income. Or, to a man living on "immoral earnings", perhaps all three.

screwy: Daft.

scuffer: A police officer of any rank.

Derived perhaps from "scuffler"; one who causes or takes part in scuffles.

scuppered: Defeated, finished with, done for. **'e orter be 'ung, drawn an' scuppered:** He should be punished. The word is adopted from the merchant navy.

sea-pie: Scouse.

seatworms: Word mumbled in mock-apology when scratching one's backside in public.

seein' as 'ow yer twistin' me arm: Mock-modest way of accepting an offer, usually of a drink of beer.

seen: Saw. As in **'e done it—I seen 'im.**

see that wet?: I am about to tell the truth.

Derived from a jingle recited after licking a finger: "See that wet, see that dry?—cut me froat if I tell a lie!"

see ther light: To plead guilty or to reform.

segs: Areas of thickened skin resembling large corns. **got segs on 'is arse** is said of a lazy, shiftless person, a work-dodger, or someone kept waiting.

setts: Granite road-blocks. **'e dented ther setts:** He fell heavily.

sex: Wot they put thar coal in in Blendellsahnds (a posh suburb of Liverpool).

Sexy Bloke: A snooper; an inquisitive person. As in **'e' thinks 'e's Sexy Bloke.**

For once unconnected with sex; derived from "Sexton Blake", the fictional detective.

sharp as a pickled 'erring: Said of a clever fellow; a wise guy.

sharpy 'arpy: A businesslike woman; a calculating female; a girl on the make.

shebeen: Any place in which liquor is sold illegally, usually at an extortionate price. Now legally superseded by clubs.

she got it from ther coal-man: Sardonic comment implying that the father of the expected child is not known. Other similar phrases are: **she got it from ther Pru; she got guv it behind an 'oarding** (a bill-board); **she got guv it under a tripe-stall; she made it back o' ther boozer; she let ther**

winder-cleaner in; she found it in ther bull-rushes; only way she could pay ther tally-man, etc., etc.

Some years ago the Co-operative Wholesale Society had to withdraw posters of a smiling housewife carrying a full shopping basket, saying "I got it at the Co-op!" when it was discovered that neighbouring posters sometimes happened to be those that warned against the dangers of venereal disease.

sherper: An ambitious person; one with his eye to the main chance. Said of an autocratic boss and his attending sycophants **'e climbs all over yer wit' 'is buncher sherpers.**

Derived from "Sherpa" and clearly adopted since the conquest of Everest.

she's got it cemented up an' hearthstoned over: Said of a girl who refuses to be seduced.

she's got one of them new uvvings an' thinks she's Lady Muck: She has a new gas or electric cooker and is very pleased with it.

she talks Blendellsahnds: Said of a woman considered to have an affected accent. The reference is to **Blundellsands,** a residential area north of Liverpool.

Other similar phrases are "she talks cut glass"; "talks like Lady Muck of Muck Hall"; "talks like a shillun in ther Co-op"; "got nine outer ten at skule", etc., etc.

shifter: A removal man.

shiftin': Moving to another address.

shindig: A dance; a party that includes a dance. As in **they 'ad a whizzo shindig after ther wedd'n'.**

shindy: An argument, dispute or fight. To **kick up a shindy:** to start a row.

shin off: Go away; get to hell out of it.

ship's Mary: An effeminate man or a male prostitute.

Shit Creek: The River Mersey.

Sailors' slang; from the sometimes less than effective disposal of sewage into the Mersey by local authorities.

shit-'ot: Very good, excellent, wonderful.

shit-scairt: Badly frightened.

shittus: A lavatory.

A slight corruption of two Anglo-Saxon words that were once perfectly respectable. Lavatory is one of many inaccurate euphemisms.

shoe nuts: Oleo nuts, used in the manufacture of margarine. This name arises from their fancied

resemblance to clogs.
Cf. also "Cashew Nuts".

shoplifters' express: Any day excursion train from the surrounding countryside to Liverpool.

shortarsed: Of small stature.

shute: A dangerous metal channel down which heavy packages and crates are slid. Hence **up ther shute:** To be in serious trouble. **'e's got 'er up ther shute:** He has made her pregnant.

singin' in ther rain: Pretending that things are better than they are; disregarding trouble; procrastinating.

sinner club: A synagogue.

sin-shifter: A parson, priest or rabbi.

skimmer or **skipper:** A small, flat stone or piece of slate.

skinny: Mean, parsimonious. **skinny-arsed bastard:** A very mean person.

skint: Penniless. As in **we 'ad a session at ther boozer an' I come out skint.**

skin ther dog: To encourage a person to spend all his money on drink.

skellington: A skeleton. **she's gone down ter a skellington** is said of a woman who has been very ill. **I'll leave yer me skellington** (in my will): You will get nothing out of me.

Skem: The township of **Skelmersdale**, Lancashire.

skule: A school. **Are yez goin' ter skule terday?** A **street-skule** is a group of gamblers playing pitch-and-toss.

Sometimes also called "An Open Air Prayer Meeting" because a group of men cast their eyes upwards, then look down and murmur, "Aw Christ".

sling yer 'ook: Clear off; go away. The reference is to a docker's loading-hook.

slobbergob: Name given to a person with a thick-lipped, drooling kind of mouth.

slog: To work hard. **a rill slog**: A difficult or tiring job. Said of a bullying boss **'e'd 'ave me sloggin' all day an' 'alf ther bloody night.**

slop: A police constable.

Sloppy Joe: A careless, shiftless person.

smart: Well, healthy. Used in a negative sense as in

no, I ain't too smart terday, meaning not very well.

smellin' down grids: The technique of falling ill. Said of a child **'e's picked up a gairm somewhurs —'e muster bin smellin' down grids.**

smoked Irishman: A Negro, a coloured person.
Also "Spade" or "Blammo".

snadger: A house sparrow. **couldn't kick a snadger up its arse** is said of a person considered weak and ineffectual.

Snellens: The borough of **St. Helens,** Lancashire.

sniff up, yer in ther cunny: Enjoy the fresh country air.

snitch: To steal. Also to tell tales or to betray someone. **A dairty snitch:** A tale-bearer; a traitor.

snot fur: Anything considered wrong or unfair; an injustice. As in **I tell yer it snot fur.**

snot pie: Cowheel pie, a glutinous concoction typifying Northern fondness for offal.

snot pudden: Sago or tapioca pudding.

Snotty Bash: A Bootle term for the district of **Knotty Ash,** Liverpool.

snout: Tobacco, especially when smuggled into prison. **snout-king:** a prison tobacco-trader. **snout** can also mean nose as in **'ow'd yer like a bang on ther snout?**: an invitation to a fight.

snucked: Past tense of to sneak, meaning to smuggle. As in **I snucked it in from 'Ong Kong.**

soady batch: Welsh soda-bread.

soak: To beg or borrow. As in **can I soak yer fer a coupler bob?**

Soapville: The district of **Port Sunlight.**

Sodom-on-ther-Liffey: The city of **Dublin.**

soggy: Dilapidated, worn out. **A soggy dump:** a dirty, tumbledown place. **A soggy do:** A disappointing and inferior affair. A mispronunciation of **saggy.**

some feller I don' know ast me ter look after it fer 'im: This is another favourite excuse for being found in possession of a stolen article.

so pissed she fell outer ther sharrer: Very drunk indeed.

"Sharrer" derived from charabanc, or excursion motor coach.

sort out: To pick a fight. As in **I kin sort yer out wit' one 'and in me kecks.**

so sharp 'e can cut putty: Said of a person who thinks himself very clever.

spit blood: An expression of impatience or anger. As in **when I think of it I could spit blood.**

sporran: Pubic hair.

sprout: A boy scout.

squashies: Broken, squashed or misshapen chocolates sold cheaply. At one time a Scouser child's dream of paradise was three-pennyworth of **squashies.**

squatter: A lavatory pan. **'e sits fer ars** (hours) **on ther squatter mumblin' to hisself.**

The plural, "squatters", means people who move into condemned property before it can be demolished, sometimes in the hope of jumping the queue for a corporation house.

squidge: To look at; to examine. As in **let's 'ave a squidge at it.** A mispronunciation of **squint.**

stand back an' let ther dog see ther rabbit: Make room.

Stan Ther: Stanley Road, Liverpool, or occasionally the **Stanley Hospital,** according to context.

starved: Very cold. **aw cheese, I'm bloody starved:** I am very cold.

stash: To put, place or hide.

stickjaw: A glutinous form of toffee. **give 'im some stickjaw:** Tell him to shut up.

stick-man: A carefully dressed and very dapper individual; a fusspot.

Derived from a onetime Army practice of presenting a stick to the smartest-looking soldier on morning parade, which article exempted him from fatigues for the rest of the day. The implication of the name is that the fussy dresser is trying to get out of something.

stuffin': Horse-hair, or flock, as used in mattresses; also a mixture of stale bread and herbs etc. which is supposed to be stuffed into cheap cuts of meat to make it go further as well as to impart a flavour.

In practice, however, it is often cooked separately (like the so-called crust of alleged pies). Hence servers at cafeterias usually make a point of asking, " Yer want stuffin'?", a question which is often parried with some fitting repartee.

sturs: Stairs. A catch-phrase is **get up them sturs**, being an invitation to an amorous exercise.

Sudner: Anyone whose speech suggests that he comes from a town in the south of England, such as Chester.

sufrin crise: An ejaculation more emphatic than **flippin 'eck**.

sunbeams: Children who regularly attend Sunday School or adults who are persistent church-goers.
Derived from "Jesus wants me for a sunbeam".

summings: A summons. As in **this 'ere slop brung me a summings an' I gotter go ter court.** Also **a blue paper**.

sup: To drink. Many Scousers judge a man's character and worth by his capacity for drink. As in **aye, 'e's a good lad is Joe—'e can sup ale**.

sweat on, to: To wait anxiously for a given result. A too-willing worker is said to be **sweat'n' on promotion**.

Sweeny: A barber. **I'm goin' ter Sweeny ter 'ave me hur cut.** Derived from **Sweeny Tod**.

swipe: To confiscate or steal. **'Oo's ther bastard what swiped me moo?** Who is the person who has stolen the milk?

T

take 'is kecks down, to: To put a person in his place; to expose somebody.

take ther can back, to: To accept the responsibility; to suffer the blame. As in **I ain't goin' ter take ther can back fer 'im.**

take yer jacket off: This invitation to a fight usually is made in the hope that the victim can be knocked senseless while his arms are still trapped in his sleeves.

talk wet, to: To indulge in pointless or stupid conversation; to make silly remarks.

tally-man: A collector of instalments for goods supplied on credit. **as ard as a breathless tally-man:** To be pressing and insistent.

tanrogans: Escallops. This word is of Manx origin.

tarara: A tiara. Used in an ironical sense. Said of a woman adorned with a new and flossy hat **'aw, look at Lady Muck in 'er tarara.**

tart: A girl, not necessarily of questionable character.

tatters: A walk, trip or visit. **are yez goin' fer a tatters?:** Are you going for a walk? This is baby-talk of the kind sometimes used between Scouser adults.

tatty hur: A term of mild or jocular abuse. As in **'ey you wit' ther tatty hur.**

t.b.: Well-busted. As in **that judy's got t.b.**, meaning "two beauties". Also **knockers** or **bristlers.**

tea-can: A billy-can in which tea is brewed sometimes with the aid of a blow-lamp. Hence **hotter than a bloody tea-can:** Sexually excited.

teacher's pet: A spoiled child, a milksop. Also an earnest student, a swot.

tear-arse: A busy person; one who refuses to dawdle or waste time. A go-getter.

tenpence to ther shillun: Mentally deficient; not altogether of sound mind.

terf it out: Throw it away. **I get terfed outer ther boozer:** I was thrown out of the public house.

Thairsday: Thursday. **'e don't know Thairsday**

from brekfuss-time: He is half-witted.

that's all me fat aunt: It's rubbish. I don't believe it.

that's ther God's truth: More often than not this expression is used to support a thundering lie.

As, when fending off a would-be cadger, "I ain't gotter shillun in me pairce an' that's ther God's truth".

ther likes of 'er: An expression of contempt implying that the person referred to is of a lower order of life.

Ther T'ree Burs: A fairy tale popular with Scouser toddlers too young to appreciate dirty limericks. It is about three bears.

Ther Sash Me Father Wore: Battle hymn of the **Loyal Order of Orange Lodges,** sometimes parodied as **Ther Bash Me Father 'Ad.**

they buried 'im wid 'am: He had a lavish funeral.

thick: Stupid. **so thick 'e can't leak:** Very stupid. **thick as two short planks:** Extremely stupid.

thinks 'e's 'eap big but 'e's just a big 'eap (of manure): Said of a bombastic person.

thinks 'isself a rill Stadium lad: Said of a bully

or of one who brags of his fighting ability.

The reference is to the "Liverpool Stadium", a boxing and wrestling centre, also used for promenade concerts until "Gilbert & Sullivan" appeared on posters as "Gilbert v. Sullivan".

thinks wood don't grow on trees: Said of a mean person, a skinflint.

think yer a hard skin, don'tcher?: You're not so tough!

this side o' Wigan: A term of comparison. As in **nuttin like it this side o' Wigan.**

thundermug: A chamber-pot.

This word is thought to be of American origin, although it was probably exported there from Lancashire as "the under-mug", i.e. the mug that goes under the bed.

thur's a dollop of no good ter nuttin: Said of a shiftless person, somebody considered worthless.

tickler: A joker, a humourist. As in **that feller's a rill tickler.**

tiger-nuts: European sedge-nuts, popular among children.

tight one: A parsimonious person; a penny-pincher. Also a virgin.

Tilly Mint: Whozit, whatsername. Derived from an oldtime mint-seller who peddled her wares outside St. John's Market, Liverpool.

time-bean: Momentarily. As in **thassall fer ther time bean.**

Tin-can (or **Back-Entry**) **Dribblers:** Derisory name for a bad football team.

tip: A municipal rubbish-dump. Said of something despised, such as a worn-out coat or an ancient car, **'e dug it outer ther tip.**

tip-cat: A game in which a piece of wood is rapped to make it jump and is then struck while in mid-air. Also called **bouncey, knurr and spell,** etc., etc.

tip-scrabbler: A person who searches ash-heaps for small quantities of burnable fuel.

tishy paper: Lavatory paper.

Tit Street: Milk Street, Liverpool.

tizzy: A state of excited confusion; a touch of hysteria. As in **she got inter a proper tizzy.**

tod: Alone, in solitude. **on me tod:** by myself. An

alternative phrase is **on me pat**.

Both are shortened versions of rhyming slang derived from "Tod" (or "Pat") "Malone".

tonka-beans: Tonquin beans, used in snuff-making.

tontine: A club whose members save money for holidays, Christmas or other special occasions.

From a form of life-annuity invented by Lorenzo Tonti, a Neopolitan, 1653.

too tired to tip a bloody wall-bin: Said of a person considered lazy and shiftless.

The reference is to a special type of garbage-bin built into alley walls and easily capable of being tilted outward for emptying purposes.

tosh: A neutral form of address less used than **wack** or **wacker; think yer posh, tosh, don'tcher?**

totterin' along like a hen wit' ther staggers: Said of a reeling drunkard.

t'rah well: Goodbye. Other versions are **t'rah now** and **t'rah fer now**.

From the infantile farewell "Ta-ta". Also "t'rah wack", pronounced "Sarawak".

trapped in ther tram-lines: To be placed in an

awkward predicament. This phrase, which is now dying out, arose from the frequency with which bicycle-riders were overthrown when their wheels became caught in street-car lines.

Although trams were discarded in 1957 Liverpool Corporation has preserved to this day (October 1, 1966) in South Castle Street (and probably elsewhere too) some fine sets of tramlines whose high polish vies with that of the surrounding cobblestones. It has never been explained whether this is intended to be a practice skid-pan for motorists or an incipient transport museum.

tripe-hound: A mongrel dog. Also applied to a racing greyhound that persists in putting up a disappointing performance.

turd-burglar: A homosexual.

Tyfud Murry (Typhoid Mary): An old and conspicuously dirty woman or perhaps an elderly prostitute.

U

Uni, Ther: The University of Liverpool; **uni-type:** a university student.

up ther pole: Crazy, irresponsible.

up ther shute: In serious trouble. Other similar phrases are **up ther cooee; up ther drain; up ther creek,** etc., etc.

upyer!: A term of defiance and/or contempt, but often made jocularly. Other similar phrases are **upyer pipe; upyer spout; upyer geezik; upyer conga; upyer grommett.** The latter is of Australian origin.

us: Me. **give us a pill, wack:** Please give me a cigarette.

Utty: Utting Avenue, Liverpool. **'e's gone ter Utty fer a butty:** I'm not telling you where he has gone.

uvving: An oven, usually in the sense of a gas or electric cooker. **she's got a pudden in ther uvving:** She is pregnant.
See "Pudden Club".

V

Vale, Ther: Walton Vale to Liverpool north-enders, **Aigburth Vale** to south-enders, **St. Domingo Vale** to in-betweeners.

very close veins: Varicose veins. As in **me docter sez I got very close veins.**

Other Merseypropisms (a word coined by Stan Kelly) vouched for by a doctor in Liverpool 8 include "I'm Reece's negative, doctor", and "Consecrated Peppermint Water".

Voxey: Vauxhall Road, Liverpool.

W

wairk: Work. As in **that feller's allus outer wairk**.

wack or **wacker**: A neutral form of address used by one Scouser to another, as in **whur's yer goin, wack? wack** can also mean a portion or share, as in **yer've 'ad yer wack, wack**.
See Foreword to "Lern Yerself Scouse".

Waldorf Astoria, Ther: Walton Jail.

Wallasey Lad, a: A homosexual.
After a notorious scandal in that township many years ago.

wasserdoo?: What is the matter? As in **wasserdoo— wuz she lyin' on yer shert?**: Why are you late this morning?

wasser marrer witchew?: What is the matter with you? When this is uttered in a hoarse shout it warns of an impending assault.

wassup widger fly?: What is the matter with your trouser buttons? This question may be used for diverting the other person's attention at a critical moment, sometimes for the purpose of getting in the first blow. Another way of achieving the same desirable effect is to say urgently **'ey you, yer fly's undid.**

watch it, mate: This is a cocky challenge growled by Scouser youths, invariably when they outnumber the opposition.

Waterloo Cup, Ther: A greyhound race held at Altcar, north of Liverpool. Said of a worker who frequently absents himself on petty pretexts **'e'd take a day off fer ther Waterloo Cup.**

wayo: Wait a moment.

well, 'e knows two letters, b an' f: Said of a person for whom there is little else to be said.

The implication: "He's a bloody fool".

well 'umped an' poorly clad: Liverpool recipe for keeping the wife faithful.

wellies: Gumboots. **put on yer wellies else yer'll catch yer death** (of cold).

Cf. also Desert Wellies or Jesus Boots: sandals.

Welsh letter: A defective contraceptive.

Based on the folk-joke about a rubber sheath "wit' a leek in it". A "Scotch Letter", therefore, is the same object having been repaired.

wenner they goin' ter do summat fer ther wairkers?: This is a standard cry raised at public meetings, often by persons who have been avoiding work for years.

went out like a bleed'n' light: fainted suddenly.

wet nelly: A square-shaped, cheap type of cake thinly smeared with jam and occasionally sprinkled with dessicated coconut.

Originally called a "Nelson" cake.

wet sod: A futile talker; a thorough bore.

wheel 'im in: A catch-phrase meaning "here he is, the feeble fellow".

wheshittus?: Where is the lavatory?

Five words contracted into one, perhaps in haste.

whip: To confiscate or steal. As in **'e whipped it from Clarry (Clarence Dock).**

However, a "whip-round" is a subscription of cash made by several persons for a given purpose, usually a colleague's misfortune such as a lost pay packet.

whip behind: Warning cry shouted by children at carters when other children are stealing rides by hanging on the back.

whistle: A ship's siren.

Whizbang Winnie: A woman motorist.

whizzo: Good, excellent. Usually employed in an ironical sense.

wide as Lime Street: Of a cunning person.

whoof: To pass wind; also **whoof like a booze-moke.**

whur yer off?: Quo Vadis?

whur's yer bin?: Where have you been?

> It is said that a garbage collector once called at a Liverpool house and asked the occupant, "whur's yer bin?", meaning the dust-bin. And the man replied "I jes' bin upsturs—whur's you bin?"

whur's yer gogs (spectacles): Why can't you see; why don't you understand?

wick: A penis. **gets on me wick:** Annoys me very much.

Willum pur: A William pear.

Windy 'ill: James Street, Liverpool, which slopes towards the Pier Head and catches prevailing winds.

winge: To cry wearily and persistently. A Scouser mother's angry shout sometimes is **if yer don't stop wingeing I'll knock yer bloody 'ead off.**

Composite of "wail and cringe".

winnuck or **winnick:** Daft, dotty. As in **yer better watch that feller, 'e's winnuck.**

Derived from the County Mental Hospital at Winwick, Lancashire.

wooden lecher: I won't permit it. As in **mebbe yer think yer can but I wooden lecher.**

woozey: Weak, faint. As in **I come over all woozey-like.**

wrap it up: Shut up, give it a rest; **wrap it up an' I'll take it wimme:** Sarcastic response to a silly suggestion.

wreck ther wake, to: To start a fight among mourners, perhaps by mentioning that the deceased expired without having paid his debts.

Y

Yackaw! Yakspraze! or **Eggseeiecho!**: Oldtime street cry of Merseyside newsboys, literally **Echo! Express!**

Now that the "Express has been absorbed by "The Liverpool Echo" the cry has degenerated into the "Caw! Caw!" of a crow with a bad cold.

yak: To nag; to keep up a running fire of criticism.

yeard thissun?: Not a question but the introduction to a dirty joke.

yer back wheel's goin' round: Distracting information howled by Scouser children at passing cyclists.

yer broke yer mother's 'eart but yer won't break mine: I refuse to bother about you.

yer can stuff it: I don't want it; you can keep it.

yer got ther price uvver cupper tea?: This is the standard approach of street cadgers. Money, if given, usually is spent on beer.

yer'd need six men an' a special blessin': Contemptuous answer to a challenge to a fight.

yer up agen ther shittus: You are in a difficult position.

An alternative, more rural, phrase is "yer up agen ther midden".

yer wha'?: Literally **you what?** I beg your pardon, what did you say?

yez aren't takin' 'im in: This is the frenzied shout of the Scouser when his boozing-pal is being arrested.

yimkin: Nonsense; I don't believe it.

This is of Arabic origin.

ying-tong: Oriental music. Also a disjointed, erratic dance. **'e were doin' a ying-tong when ther scuffers 'auled 'im in**: He was doing a drunken dance when the police arrested him.

yocker: to spit.

See also "golly".

yowler: A cat. **jowler-yowler**: An alley cat.

yunnuck: Frigid; not interested in sex. **'e wooden take a blind bit o' notice of 'er, 'e's a rill yunnucky bastard.**

Possibly a mispronunciation of "eunuch".

Z

Ziggie: Zig-Zag Road—where Mrs. Bessie Braddock, M.P., lives.

An Everyday History of Liverpool & Merseyside

This is a fascinating chronicle of everyday events in Liverpool and Merseyside down the centuries, a reprint of the cumulative history first begun by the 18th-century Liverpool publisher, John Gore. He gleaned the earlier material from ancient chronicles and archives, and then from the many local newspapers the town and city supported. Previously published in two volumes, this Everyday History has now been reissued in an enlarged single volume, with a full-colour fold-out cover showing the old Liverpool waterfront as it was in 1835, with numerous archival illustrations, some of them never before published. The Everyday History is indispensable for the study of Local History in schools and universities, and for those researching their family history, as it establishes the dates of important events, such as the endowment of schools, the consecration of churches, the laying-out of parks, cemeteries and and other public spaces, as well as the erection of all the notable buildings, civic and private. And those amazing innovations! In 1899 a 130 mph inter-city elevated monorail was being planned to run between Liverpool and Manchester; and by 1854 a public electric clock had been installed in Castle Street.

Available from your bookshop, or (by post only) from Scouse Press

Merseyside at War (Rodney Whitworth)
Bombers over Merseyside The 1942 story.
(Two inspirational histories of the wartime Blitz)
Liverpool and Slavery (by 'Dicky Sam' 1884)
Liverpool's First Street Directory (1766)
(Who were your ancestors, where did they live?)

LIVERPOOL PACKETS

A series of collections of Local History material - maps, documents, plans, postcards, prints and views.

No.1 Liverpool Ballads, Broadsides and Sea Songs.
No. 2 Maps, Plans and Views - earliest times to 1830.
No. 2+2 Maps, Plans and Views - 1830 to 1980s.
No. 3 Merseyside Transport: buses, trams, ferries etc.
No. 4 Liverpool-Manchester Railway 1830.
No. 5 Liverpool Slavers and Privateers.
No. 7 Liverpool Shipping through the Ages.
No. 10 Prehistoric & Roman Merseyside.
No. 14 John Berbiers's Merseyside in the 1950s.
No. 15 Sing the Titanic! An Instant Grief Kit of 1912: including a Casette of 11 tracks of contemporary songs and verse commemorating the worst-ever sea disaster.

Send a SAE for a list of Books, Packets, Prints, Postcards and Historic Maps of Merseyside to Scouse Press, Liverpool L8 3SB
Telephone 0151-727 2727 Facsimile 0151-727 7272
email: ingrid.scousepress@talktalk.net

MAPS OF LIVERPOOL AND MERSEYSIDE
the famous Scouse Press reprints
Look for this stamp

They include maps and plans from the middle ages, ca.1350 AD to the 1600s, to Chadwick's 1725 'Map of all the Streets and Lanes'; John Eyes's Plan of 1765; Yates & Perry's of 1768; Charles Eyes 1785; Stockdale's Plan of Liverpool 1795; Wilkes's Map of the Wirral, 'Wallisey, Bromborrow, Bebbington', etc. of 1801; The Hundred of Wirral 1820; Thomas Kaye's Plan of 1810; Swire 1823/4; and town maps and street plans from the 1850s to the 1930s, including the Godfrey Edition Ordance Survey; also spectacular panoramic bird's-eye views, etc. etc. etc.

Please send a stamped/addressed envelope for a complete and up-to-date list.